THE HEB DISCIPLESHIP MANUAL VOLUME II

Bread of the Word

Dr Trevor Udennis DD

Copyright © 2017

1st Edition 2017

THE HEBREW DISCIPLESHIP MANUAL VOLUME II

Copyright © 2017 by Dr Trevor Udennis
First published in the UK by EasyRway Ltd 2017
1st Edition
www.Hebrewapostolic.com

All scripture quotations in this publication are from the King James Authorised Version of the Holy Bible 'Please note emphasis where added to scriptures'

Printed in the USA
First Printing 2017

by Dr. Trevor H. Udennis D.D.

ISBN-13: 978-0956490650 (EasyRway Ltd)
ISBN-10: 0956490654

Dedication

This book is first dedicated to Elohim the giver of life and inspiration without whom this work would not exist. Secondly my thanks goes out to my family: Julia my wife and my two sons (Theron and Danel). They are so supportive of my work and ministry that I can only acknowledge them with the deepest of thanks to Elohim.

This book is further dedicated to the memory of Sister Lucita Marcelle who so tirelessly helped me to type and set in order the original manuscripts from which this book is written. It is also dedicated to Sis. Susan Charles who bugged me to complete this series so that she could receive the biblical support she required.

If you have further questions, contact EasyRway Ltd. Our regular business hours are Mon-Thurs. 9:30 am – 6 pm GMT, and Friday 10:30 am – 5 pm. During these hours, you can reach us by phone, or email. Outside of these hours, either call and leave a message or email us.

Email: hebrewapostolic@gmail.com

Website www.hebrewapostolic.com

Contents

Foreword

This book was written as a follow on from the book, "Black skin royal identity" which came about due to the needs of Hebrews for a revelation and understanding of their identity.

In this series of books, we take another step by unwrapping teaching that enables a Hebrew to master the Book that belongs to them, for "The Bible" is not a gentile book, but a book given by Elohim to His people. So to equip Hebrew Apostolics with the knowledge that is required to develop scholarship and skill in their hereditary faith the writer has offered this series of books to disciple the Hebrew believer whether new to the faith or a seasoned believer, so that there is something for every level of maturity.

This series is also designed to help pastors to develop the work of Yah more systematically by providing them with the tools they need so that they do not need to waste time developing them or work in a hit and miss way to achieve the results that Yah desires to give to them.

In volume 1 you will encounter the, "Milk of the Word" or a basic orientation to the faith that will allow you to get the information that will enable you to gain the basic knowledge required to stand steadfast in the faith.

In volume 2 (this book) you can expect to learn stronger doctrine (teaching) that will give you a strong foundation and higher level of understanding of the important teachings in the Bible.

Volume 3 is all about leadership and ministerial responsibilities. Volume 3 is written in order to develop the ability of the ministers of the people of Yah to deliver excellent leadership and representation. They are expected to grow from simple leaders of tens to those with greater capacity, to lead hundreds and even thousands.

Volume 4 looks at how we can simplify the administration of the work of Yah by implementing simple systems and processes that ensure we are able to maintain order and deliver excellence. While making it clear that good administration is not an optional alternative, it's imperative.

Lastly, in volume 5 we examine and establish the system of outreach and missionary approach that was used by the apostle Paul and others that works.

This has one purpose; so that we can implement it to awaken Hebrew apostolics all over the world and in so doing hasten the return of our Yah and Saviour Yahoshuah our Messiah.

Introduction

This book is not meant to read as a novel. It is a handbook that is meant for study. So as you do each lesson, make notes in the book about things you do not understand that requires further study.

This book is designed to disciple the reader and make them strong and knowledgeable about the beliefs of the apostles and disciples of Yahoshuah Messiah.

Make notes about things that require you to ask questions, highlight revelations that are given to you and keep a record of what you have learned.

The information is as far as possible done in a systematic way, but this work is by no means totally complete as there is only so much that can go in one book.

As you go through this book, bear in mind that the information is graded and there are audio or video lessons that can be used along-side the book to help your understanding.

Finally each chapter comes with summaries and discussions. At the very end of the book there is a multiple choice test that allows the reader to see how well they have assimilated the information.

May Elohim bless you as you, "Study to show yourself approved unto Elohim, a workman that needeth not to be ashamed, rightly dividing the Word of truth" **2 Timothy 2:15**.

Chapter One

THE BIBLE AND ALL OF ITS AUTHORITY

Memory Verse

Psalm 119:160 *"Thy word is true from the beginning: and every one of thy righteous judgments endureth for ever"*

Introduction

If you take a look at **Acts 2:22-37**, *"Ye men of Israel, hear these words; Jesus of Nazareth, a man approved of God among you by miracles and wonders and signs, which God did by him in the midst of you, as ye yourselves also know: Him, being delivered by the determinate counsel and foreknowledge of God, ye have taken, and by wicked hands have crucified and slain: Whom God hath raised up, having loosed the pains of death: because it was not possible that he should be* *holden of it.*

For David speaketh concerning him, I foresaw the Lord always before my face, for he is on my right hand, that I should not be moved: Therefore did my heart rejoice, and my tongue was glad; moreover also my flesh shall rest in hope: Because thou wilt not leave my soul in hell, neither wilt thou suffer thine Holy One to see corruption. Thou hast made known to me the ways of life; thou shalt make me full of joy with thy countenance.

Men and brethren, let me freely speak unto you of the patriarch David, that he is both dead and buried, and his sepulchre is with us unto this day. Therefore being a prophet, and knowing that God had sworn with an oath to him, that of the fruit of his loins, according to the flesh, he would raise up Christ to sit on his throne; He seeing this before spake of the resurrection of Christ, that his soul was not left in hell, neither his flesh did see corruption.

This Jesus hath God raised up, whereof we all are witnesses. Therefore being by the right hand of God exalted, and having received of the Father the promise of the Holy Ghost, he hath shed forth this, which ye now see and hear. For David is not ascended into the heavens: but he saith himself,

The Lord said unto my Lord, Sit thou on my right hand, Until I make thy foes thy footstool. Therefore let all the house of Israel know assuredly, that God hath made the same Jesus, whom ye have crucified, both Lord and Christ. Now when they heard this, they were pricked in their heart, and said unto Peter and to the rest of the apostles, Men and brethren, what shall we do?"

You will find in the scripture above, how Peter preached about Jesus to a crowd of people who had come running to see what was happening when the first believers were filled with the Holy Spirit.

As the crowd heard about the coming of Yahoshuah, the Son of Elohim and his life, his death at the hands of their leaders, and his resurrection and Lordship at Elohim's right hand, they asked Peter an important question ~ What Shall We Do?

Peter's answers in **Acts 2.38** *"Then Peter said unto them, Repent, and be baptized every one of you in the name of Jesus Christ for the remission of sins, and ye shall receive the gift of the Holy Ghost."* This tells us the three important things that are required for entrance into Elohim's spiritual family or Kingdom.

A. Repent of your sins

B. Be baptised into the name of Yahoshuah

C. Receive the gift of the Holy Ghost the way they did on the day of Pentecost.

Acting on the authority of Elohim's Word

We should be sure that whatever we do, because it's in line with His Word, it is right. However it is then also empowering. Because we are empowered through the Word to fulfil what Elohim has said we are to do.

He will therefore stand with us and by us, to ensure that His Word is fulfilled, because the Word has been given all authority and is backed up by all of His authority and power. The Bible is Elohim's Word recorded on paper or electronically.

The English word Bible comes from a Greek word meaning "the books". It is more than a book, it is sixty six books. Yet more than just "The Book" it is also called "The Word of God" because it is Elohim's very Word to the human race.

That name is accurate as it contains Elohim's clear words or instructions to man. It does not just contain what Elohim says, it is "the Word of God". **Psalms 40:7**, *"Then said I, Lo, I come: in the volume of the book it is written of me"*

PRINCIPLE 1 - THE BIBLE IS THE WORD OF GOD

1 Thessalonians 2:13, *"For this cause also thank we God without ceasing, because, when ye received the word of God which ye heard of us, ye received it not as the word of men, but as it is in truth, the word of God, which effectually worketh also in you that believe."* -- The bible is not the word of man **1Peter 1:25**, *"But the word of the Lord endureth for ever. And this is the word which by the gospel is preached unto you."* **(Psalms 119:105; 2 Peter 1:19).**

It must be clear that Elohim's word the Bible is above our dreams, visions, personal beliefs and experiences. When those conflicts with Elohim's word He is right and we are wrong and we must defer to His Word. **Jeremiah 23:29**, *"Is not my word like as a fire? saith the Lord; and like a hammer that breaketh the rock in pieces?"* **(Hebrews 4:12).**

There are Sixty-six books in the Bible. The Bible is split into 2 halves called Testaments. The word testament means covenant, contract and agreement.

The Old Testament has 39 books:-

1. Genesis - Deuteronomy are called the Pentateuch or Laws. Joshua - Esther are 12 Historical books.

2. Job - Songs of Solomon are 5 Poetry books

3. Isaiah - Malachi are 17 Prophecy books

The New Testament which has 27 books:-

1. The first four are called the Gospels. Then there is:-1 Historical book – the book of Acts

2. There are 21 Epistles – From Romans to Jude

3. Last but not least is the final book which is one of Prophecy - Revelations

PRINCIPLE 2 - ELOHIM WROTE THE BIBLE

In writing the Bible, Elohim used 40 men over a period of 1,600 years. Although men were used over time, it is quite evident from its content and flow that the Bible has only one author. The Bible is the product of one master mind, ELOHIM.

Elohim wrote the Bible by direct inspiration like a manager writes through a secretary. **2 Timothy 3:16**, *"All scripture is given by inspiration of*

God, and is profitable for doctrine, for reproof, for correction, for instruction in righteousness:"

If every scripture is inspired by Elohim, then there can be no scripture which isn't inspired by Elohim. Inspiration means 'Elohim breathed'. No prophecy of scripture will be found to come from the prophet's (Elohim's mouthpiece in human form) own imagination or prompting.

2 Peter 1:20-21, *"Knowing this first, that no prophecy of the scripture is of any private interpretation. For the prophecy came not in old time by the will of man: but holy men of God spake as they were moved by the Holy Ghost."* The moral standards of the Bible prove it to be divine**. 1 Peter 1:16**, *"Because it is written, Be ye holy; for I am holy"*.

PRINCIPLE 3 - THE BIBLE IS THE SUPREME AUTHORITY IN ALL THE AFFAIRS OF LIFE

The word is Elohim's character while His name is His identity. **Psalm 18:30**, *"As for God, his way is perfect: the word of the Lord is tried: he is a buckler to all those that trust in him."* The word is also final - **Luke 21:33**, *"Heaven and earth shall pass away: but my words shall not pass away."*

The word is truth **John 17:17**, *"Sanctify them through thy truth: thy word is truth."* **(Romans 3:4)**. The word is important as it's the difference

19

between life and death because it will judge you one day.

<u>John 12:48</u>, *"He that rejecteth me, and receiveth not my words, hath one that judgeth him: the word that I have spoken, the same shall judge him in the last day."* **(Matthew 4:4).**

PRINCIPLE 4 - THE BIBLE IS A BOOK ABOUT PURPOSE AND DESTINY

Hearing it gives faith to save your soul. **<u>Romans 10:17</u>**, *"So then faith cometh by hearing, and hearing by the word of God."*

It will make you wise unto salvation. **<u>2 Timothy 3:15</u>**, *"And that from a child thou hast known the Holy Scriptures, which are able to make thee wise unto salvation through faith which is in Christ Jesus."* The Scripture is profitable for 4 things: Doctrine, reproof, correction, instruction in righteousness.

The Bible will change the soul. **<u>Psalm 19:7</u>**, *"The law of the Lord is perfect, converting the soul: the testimony of the Lord is sure, making wise the simple."*

Those who do not believe or teach the word of God have a shock in store. **<u>1 Timothy 5:24,</u>** *"Some men's sins are open beforehand, going before to judgment; and some men they follow*
20

after"

PRINCIPLE 5 - THE BIBLE CAN BE LEARNED BY VARIOUS METHODS

i. Study   **(2 Timothy 2:15)**

ii. Search **(John 5:39)**

iii. Read **(Matthew 21:42)**

iv. Adoption and intentional learning **(Matthew 11:29)**

v. Careful application of what you do understand **(Psalm 119:11)**

vi. Meditate (Joshua 1:8)

We must have the right attitude to scripture**. Acts 17:11**, *"These were more noble than those in Thessalonica, in that they received the word with all readiness of mind, and searched the scriptures daily, whether those things were so."*

PRINCIPLE 6 - THE BIBLE IS ITS OWN BEST INTERPRETER

In the mouth of two or three witnesses interpretation and judgements are established or safely made.

Matthew 18:16, *"But if he will not hear thee, then take with thee one or two more, that in the mouth of two or three witnesses every word may* *be established".* Prove everything throw away the bad and keep the good.

1Thessalonians 5:21, *"Prove all things; hold fast that which is good";* **(2 Corinthians 12:1; Deuteronomy 17:6).**

Only accept teaching that can be traced to the apostles and disciples of Yahoshuah. **2 John 1:10**, *"If there come any unto you, and bring not this doctrine, receive him not into your house, neither bid him God speed".*

Don't accept private interpretations **(2 Peter 1:20).** To find the true definition of a particular term in scripture why not conduct a word study (Etymology).

Taking the scripture mentioned before in **Acts 2:37**, the question is, "What must we do?" or put another way, "What do we need to do to be saved?" The instructions are then given. So if we obey the instructions, what will be the result? The answer is that we will be saved.

On what authority? The authority of the Word of Elohim. He gives us His Word, we obey and we get the results that He promised. This is how it works in every case. Elohim says, we obey or disobey and receive the reward for how we have acted within or outside of the authority of the Words of Elohim.

2 Timothy 3:16-17 *"All scripture is given by inspiration of God, and is profitable for doctrine, for reproof, for correction, for instruction in righteousness: That the man of God may be perfect, throughly furnished unto all good works"* That scripture above says you are equipped or empowered to do good things or good works through the scriptures. Why? Because the Word has the full authority of Elohim behind it.

Listen to this: **2 Peter 1: 20-21,** *"Knowing this first, that no prophecy of the scripture is of any private interpretation. For the prophecy came not in old time by the will of man: but holy men of God (Elohim) spake as they were moved by the Holy Ghost."*

Belief in the Word is central to demonstrating trust for Elohim – "Hath God said?" was the accusation of the devil. So without believing and accepting the Bible (Elohim) as the Word of Elohim, no-one can trust Elohim, we either follow Elohim through His Word and be saved or reject Elohim by ignoring His Word and be lost.

If then the Bible is true, it's either all true or Elohim is a liar. If Elohim is a liar then you cannot trust Him and therefore cannot follow Him.

It's a circular argument, which makes trust essential to the authority that the Word has in our lives and how faithfully we implement it or unfaithfully neglect it.

23

If indeed the Bible is true, then that makes Elohim true (to the individual believer not necessarily all people) and everything Elohim says is also true even if others don't believe Him.

- Therefore Heaven and hell is real

- Salvation is real

- The results of not being saved are real

- And the world to come is real

So then, that means we have a whole new standard for life and living which must be respected before it can be experienced. This standard is living by faith in Elohim's Words; **Hebrews 11:6,** *"But without faith it is impossible to please him: for he that cometh to God (Elohim) must believe that he is, and that he is a rewarder of them that diligently seek him"*

To truly believe Elohim's Word, you must know what it says, as ignorance damns you to relying upon others to deliver or explain what they may not understand or even know. This was the problem with Eve, she was deceived because she did not know what Elohim had said for herself.

So having an overview of the Bible and your history can help you to further acknowledge the Word of Elohim and establish you in your full historic identity as a Hebrew. History is valid in so far as it agrees with the Bible, for the Bible is His-story.

Overview of the contents of the Bible

1. Creation

2. The fall

3. The flood

4. The tower of Babel

5. The patriarchs

6. Israel in Egypt - Slavery

7. Ten Commandments and the tabernacle

8. Wilderness transition

9. Conquest of the land

10. Judges and kings

11. Saul, David, Solomon

12. The divided Kingdom

13. Assyrian and Babylonian Crisis - Cyrus says Go home

14. Prophets - people of crisis

15. 400 years of silence

16. Birth of Jesus

17. Life, crucifixion, resurrection

18. Pentecost and beyond

Creation – The Earth is recreated or restored from an unexplained problem, Animals etc. are created and finally mankind is created out of the dust of the ground and the life of Elohim is breathed into him so that he becomes a living soul. Woman is taken out of man and they are called Adam.

The fall - Woman is deceived and so falls into sin, while man sins with his eyes wide open and thereby takes the entire human race that is in him but yet unborn into sin also.

As man is a slave to sin, all humans become sinners or slaves also. Think about it, slaves can only give birth to slaves. Then both the slave and his children will continue to be slaves unless something drastic happens to change the situation they find themselves in.

The flood – Elohim looked at mankind and saw the sin nature had made them disobedient. He further saw the incursion of angels and the corruption of man's DNA.

In that old world, he found only one man and his family that were without this corruption. He helped him to build an ark and take samples to preserve life, Elohim then sent a flood and wiped the slate so to speak and started again.

At Babel – Men worked together against the clear command of Elohim to overspread the Earth and populate it again. So Elohim confounded their languages according to their families so that they could no longer communicate and His purpose was achieved. The basic families led to basic language groups that are Semitic (Hebrew based), Hamitic (African languages) and Japhetic (European languages).

The Patriarchs – Then came Abraham, Isaac, Jacob and Joseph upon whom the Hebrew race depended for its covenantal descent and continuity.

For Elohim either made covenant with them or preserved the Hebrew people by them to ensure the continuity of His people when the enemy sought to erase them from history.

Israel in Egypt – Initially Israel was favoured because of Joseph, but a king arose who did not know of Joseph and as a result enslave the Children of Israel until Elohim made him let His people go.

The Commandments and Tabernacle - Then Elohim gave them commandments some 613 precepts of the law. He gave them a means to worship Him through the tabernacle. He made them a nation, trained them to be priests, warriors and a special people.

The wilderness transition – Because of their unbelief, their time in the wilderness or time of transition for that is what it was meant to be, was longer than it should have been. For 40 years they wandered in the wilderness, because although Elohim could bring them out of Egypt in one day, it would take a lot longer to get Egypt out of them.

The conquest of the land – Elohim gave them specific instructions to conquer the land and totally destroy all the peoples they found in it. They were even to kill children and animals.

This at first seems abhorrent until you understand that the Canaanites were likely a continuation of the DNA pollution from before the flood and would infect and affect humanity as a whole unless they were destroyed.

Judges and Kings – During the time of the Judges and Kings, the people went astray from Elohim. They committed idolatry and served other gods that neither they nor their fathers knew and every man did what was right in his sight.

Saul, David and Solomon - the first kings of the people of Israel. Saul ruled for 40 years and then died. David ruled for 40 years and was the beloved of Yah except in the matter of Uriah the Hittite.

Solomon was the wisest and richest man ever to have lived, but his weakness meant that his heart was led away from Yah through the many women he loved.

The divided Kingdom - After the death of Solomon the kingdom was divided between Rehoboam and Jeroboam. Rehoboam ruled three tribes: Judah, Simeon and Levi. Jeroboam took on leadership of the 10 other tribes. The three tribe confederation became know as Judah, and the 10 tribe group as Israel.

The ABC crisis – Israel (the 10 tribes) was taken into captivity by the Assyrian Empire. Later Judah was taken into slavery by the Babylonians but were released seventy years later by the command of Cyrus the Great.

The prophets – Throughout the time leading up to captivity, captivity and after captivity, Elohim sent prophets to warn His people, encourage His people and prepare His people but they did not listen but repaid His kindness by killing His prophets.

400 years of silence – Elohim responded to His people not listening by Him not speaking. For four hundred years, His people prayed and He did not answer by dream, vision, prophet or priest.

The birth of Jesus – After 400 years, Elohim sent the voice of one crying in the darkness to go before and prepare the way of Yah.

The birth of Yahoshuah (also called Jesus) was the birth of Emmanuel or Yah. Elohim at that time took on flesh form and lived among us and that man was known as the Son of Elohim.

Life, crucifixion and resurrection of Messiah - Yahoshouah's life was a sinless life, His death for our forgiveness and freedom from sin, sickness and the curse.

His resurrection to give us new life for an old one and a new covenant in place of the old covenant, for He is the way, the truth and the life. Through Yahoshuah, Elohim has provided a way for all mankind to be saved.

Pentecost and beyond – Yahoshuah gave His disciples a message they were to preach to Hebrews first and then to the whole world, beginning at Jerusalem then Judea, the Samaria and the uttermost parts of the earth. They were to spread the Good News.

We are still in that process of spreading the Good News today and must follow the pattern of taking it to the Jew (true Hebrews) first and to the nations (gentiles) afterwards. Until the entire world has heard the message we must deliver and Messiah has returned, the job is not done.

Rightly dividing the Word

As already said, **the Bible comes in two halves** - In the first half is the Old Testament (Covenant, will or contract). In the second half is the New Testament (Covenant, will or contract).

In the Old Testament we find the stories about the Hebrew people, types, shadows, analogies and prophecies about the Messiah.

In the New Testament we find the Gospels, Acts, the Letters (Epistles) and the book of Revelations. Each group of books or book has a role to play in rightly dividing and revealing the word of Elohim:

The Gospels (The life of Yahoshuah Messiah)

The book of Acts - Gives the story of the Church and how each person can be saved. Acts is the only book that tells us the message the Church preached in order to save others and how the message was implemented practically.

The letters or Epistles tell us about how to live the saved life and contains instructions for those who were saved after the order of the Book of Acts. It is not written to tell people how to be saved and is not for anyone that has not yet been saved the way the Bible teaches.

Revelations – Tells about the things which are to come and explains the events of the last days to Elohim's people.

To rightly divide the Word of Elohim is to use the Word correctly for the right purposes, in the right context and way. So if you are looking at something in the Old Testament it cannot be applied to the time in which we now live directly except as historical information, or a type or shadow of Messiah unless it is not a prophecy or principle. Prophecy equals something yet to come and a principle equals a fixed truth that is also reflected through scripture.

So if you want to be saved, you cannot learn this information from the Old Testament, the Gospels or even in the Letters (epistles). You must go to the book of Acts for this information.

If you want to learn how to live like a believer, you cannot go to the Old Testament, the Gospels, Acts or even Revelations. You must go to the Epistles or letters to find life instructions.

If you want to know who Yahoshuah is and how He lived His life you can get information from the entire Bible but the place this kind of information is most concentrated is in the Gospels (Matthew, Mark, Luke and John).

It's kind of like having a set of bank accounts set aside for specific purposes. You must go to the savings account to save, the operational account to transact operational things and the bridging account for things that need to be bridged.

You should not go to the accounts and draw on them or put into them other than for the specific purpose for which they were set up or you will experience disorder in your finances.

When we rightly divide the Word, we go to it for the specific purpose for which it was written and get the information out that it was meant to give to us.

The Word shares information about the Messiah and His people in the Old Testament and it reveals Messiah's life and mission in the Gospels.

The Bible tells us how to be saved in the book of Acts. Clarifies how we should live the saved life once we have acted on the instructions of the book of Acts through the Letters (Epistles).

Then it reveals our future destiny and the challenges in between now and our future by the book of Revelations.

Once we understand where to go to find the correct information, we must next know how to interpret (understand or deduce) correctly what we have found out. To enable this, we use various principles of interpretation.

Principles of interpreting the Word

That the Bible is the Word of Elohim has already been established **(1Thessalonians 2:13, 1 Peter 1:25, Psalm 119:105; 2 Peter 1:19).**

That our dreams, visions, beliefs and experience are subject to Elohim's word has also been established – **Hebrews 4:12**, *"For the word of God is quick, and powerful, and sharper than any twoedged sword, piercing even to the dividing asunder of soul and spirit, and of the joints and marrow, and is a discerner of the thoughts and intents of the heart."*

Elohim wrote the Bible so do not doubt it or you doubt Him – Men were used to write it, but it's evident from the flow and content that it has only one author. The Bible was written through men, but not by men **(2 Timothy 3:16, 2 Peter 1:20-21, 1 Peter 1:16).**

The Bible is therefore its own best interpreter as also established through (Matthew 18:16) we must use witnesses from our scriptural studies that agree on the same subject as evidence for our belief.

Don't accept private interpretations or people's personal opinion as the truth (just because someone says, even if they are highly esteemed by others doesn't make them automatically right, **(2 Peter 1:20).**

The principle of first mention – Finds where a subject matter was first mentioned or began and then establishes a principle based on the first time. It then follows the thread of the subject to identify a pattern. If the principle is correct the pattern will prove it or clarify it.

Every scripture has only one interpretation - but a multiplicity of applications or uses. So in study we must separate the interpretation from any potential applications.

John 3:16, should be interpreted in the context of Yahoshuah speaking to Nicodemus about being born again. The interpretation is couched in the topic of salvation. But it could be applied to speaking about new starts in life (a possible application).

The principle of contextuality - tells us all scripture is set in a context. Therefore the context defines the meaning. All scripture has only one meaning though it may have many ways you could use or apply it.

We establish the context by reading backward as far as we need to establish the start of the conversation and forward enough to find the end of the conversation. By this we identify the context of the story or conversation.

The principle of likeness – everything is created after its own kind, and can therefore only be compared with something of its kind. Always compare like with like, apples with apples and pears with pears e.g. scriptures on salvation with other scriptures about salvation not to anything unrelated.

This means that scriptures on any subject should not be compared with scriptures of a different topic to try to establish a specific and personal interpretation.

Salvation should be compared with scriptures on the topic of salvation and not with those about food or something else. An example of bad practice is: The scripture that says, "Judas went out and hung himself **(Matthew 27:5),** and another says, "Go thou and do likewise **(Luke 10:37)."**

Some people have a practice of putting scriptures together that do not belong together and the result from doing so above is very clear. You end up hanging yourself, when that is neither the intent nor interpretation for those two scriptures which are from different contexts that are not on the same subject matter.

Only the persuaded persuade: This principle means that once you understand the interpretation of a scripture and can prove it, the acid test is whether you can persuade others to believe the interpretation that you are advancing or if their challenges cause you to question yourself and go back and study more.

Truth is a divine revelation, so don't wrestle with it, pray about it instead. Scripture is its own best interpreter, but you still need the Holy Spirit's help to understand anything from the scripture.

Truth is always in total agreement with the tone and spirit of Scripture, if you think you have found a supposed truth that doesn't appear to you to be in harmony with the rest of the Word, at this point, you need to check your understanding or revelation very carefully to ensure you have not missed it.

Truth is always well balanced and sound in its explanation. It always delivers a clear answer that makes sense when it is questioned or even interrogated.

Truth always exalts Yahoshuah Messiah

Truth always has a sanctifying effect that makes you live better than before every time. So if something you study or read does not give Yahoshuah his rightful place something is wrong. Something needs to be adjusted or addressed so that truth can have its rightful position.

Definitions and The principles of canonisation

To find the true definition of a particular word or term in scripture you may need look it up in a Bible dictionary or something like a Strong's exhaustive concordance. In order to find out what Canonization is in more depth (as it's not a biblical word).

You must look it up in a comprehensive and preferably old dictionary – essentially the word means a straight rod or measuring stick (standard) which came about for three major reasons – the spread of false doctrine, the development of false writings, and the persecution of the Church in 303 AD by Diocletian.

Principles used to establish canonization standards

1. **Authorship** – the book had to be written by an apostle or close associate.

2. **Nature of the book** – agrees with the content of the Old Testament, reflected the character and work of the Lord Jesus, and agrees with existing apostolic writings.

3. **Universality** – Book is read and practiced throughout churches in the Body of Christ

4. **Inspiration** – does the book have a spiritual

character that agrees with the Holy Spirit indwelling believers everywhere.

The Process of canonisation

This process of discussion in major meetings called Councils happened sometimes over hundreds of years.

- These thorough discussions lead to decisions that were noted and divided the body of evidence into two groups:

- Unanimously accepted works – proven and authenticated.

- Spurious or disputed works – Unproven and not accepted by the body (risky).

- In the end canonisation was a scholarly exercise dependent on discussion, evidence and decision but that doesn't mean they made all of the right decisions, or that they didn't hide stuff from the so called spurious works.

- So for the value that those works have, you may consider them to be secondary to the canonised scriptures but not totally without value.

- This is because these books other than the 66 canonised accepted books are considered by some scholars to be of spiritual significance and from our point of view may at least have historical significance if not spiritual value.

- However I cannot state strongly enough that those that fall into the disputed category, must be handled with the utmost care.

Summary

1. The authority of the Bible in our life is dependent upon our acceptance and submission to it.

2. All scripture is beneficial but not all scripture is believed and therefore not all scripture is acted upon.

3. We must know the content of scripture or we will be unable even to give an account of what we believe.

4. We must be able to rightly say where we should go in scripture for specific types of information so as to rightly divide the word.

5. Scripture can be rightly interpreted only if we use the scriptures to interpret

themselves.

6. There are varied methods whereby we may learn and study the Word of Elohim.

7. Canonisation is a process of laying down a standard set of books to accept and believe as being scripture.

8. To understand doctrine remember these truths.

9. Truth comes by divine revelation so don't wrestle with it, pray about it.

10. Next to the Holy Spirit, Scripture is the best interpreter of the Bible.

11. Bible truth is always in total agreement with the entire tone and spirit of scripture.

12. Truth is always well balanced and sound.

13. Truth always exalts Yahoshuah Messiah.

14. Truth always has a sanctifying effect in the life of a believer. It will make you live better for God every time.

Finally: The Bible is a book of Faith. It is at the same time the basis and source of our faith. There are many books, yet the world's all-time best seller in numbers and over time, is the Bible.

It's not by accident that it is printed in more languages than any other book. When correctly interpreted, the Bible never contradicts itself.

If we find a scripture that apparently contradicts some other passage of scripture, we should pray and ask the Lord for a proper understanding. As soon as we have the proper understanding there will no longer be any confusion.

Why don't you read your entire Bible, it will help you to understand its contents better. Someone said that the Bible is like a jigsaw puzzle.

The pieces begin all over the place, but as you understand the context, it's like finding the corners and edges of the puzzle. However, it takes a lifetime to fill in the pieces.

Search the scripture (take a separate piece of paper and answer the following questions:-

1. In **Exodus 24:4**, What does Moses do in response to hearing Elohim's Word?

2. In **Deuteronomy 31:11**, What does Moses command Joshua to do when the people gather together before Yah?

3. In **Joshua 1:8**, he is given personal instructions on how to prosper. What are the three steps?

4. In **Matthew 19:3-6** Yahoshuah uses the scripture to explain divorce and remarriage. What does He say about those Elohim has joined together?

5. In **Luke 17:26-32**, Does Messiah take the accounts of Noah's flood, the destruction of Sodom and Gomorrah and the calamity befalling Lot's wife literally?

6. **Acts 17:10-11** shows a specific characteristic of the Bereans that Elohim thought important to mention in the scripture, what was it?

7. What did David think a man's response to Elohim's Word should be, **Psalm 1:2**

8. In **John 5:46-47**, Yahoshuah thought that if they believed Moses, they could go a step further, what was that step?

9. **John 10:35** says something about the dependability of the scripture, what is it?

10. What has Elohim given to teach and remind us of His Word, **John 14:26.**

Discussion

1. Why should believing the Bible more important for a Hebrew, than even for a Gentile?

2. What is canonisation and how does that affect the Bible that you now own?

3. If you doubt the authenticity of the Bible, how does this affect you and those you speak to?

4. How can you practically deal with the challenges of believing in the authority of the Bible?

5. What actions do you need to take if any as a result of studying this subject matter?

Chapter Two

REPENTANCE FROM DEAD WORKS

Introduction

One definition of repentance is — turning from sin, turning to Elohim. True repentance means reflecting change that is demonstrated by a changed life.

2 Corinthians 5:17, *"Therefore if any man be in Christ, he is a new creature: old things are passed away; behold, all things are become new."*

45

This means setting your goals on the things concerning Messiah. It is the application of the will to change the heart, mind and behaviour.

These dead works are lethal because they feed the thing that keeps people from Messiah the most and which are the beliefs that they can be right without Elohim or obedience to His Word.

Repentance from sin is a mandate for survival. Yahoshuah explained that the way to eternal life was through Him, if any man rejects this way, they will perish in their sins. In this key Verse Yahoshuah says, *"Except ye repent, ye shall all likewise perish"* **Luke 13:5.**

Firstly, what is this thing called SIN? The word sin means to miss the mark and it is the cause of all the problems in the world around us. It is also the thing of which we must repent. This means it is important for us to determine exactly what is and is not sin.

Things that are not sin

TEMPTATION IS NOT SIN. Yahoshuah was tempted, but did not sin **Hebrews 4:14-15**, *"Seeing then that we have a great high priest, that is passed into the heavens, Jesus the Son of God, let us hold fast our profession. For we have not an high priest which cannot be touched with the feeling of our infirmities; but was in all points tempted like as we are, yet without sin."*

46

BREAKING ELOHIM'S WORD is sin. <u>1 John 3:4</u>, *"Whosoever committeth sin transgresseth also the law: for sin is the transgression of the law."*

NEGLECTING to do what Elohim says is good and right is SIN. <u>James 4:17</u>, *"Therefore to him that knoweth to do good, and doeth it not, to him it is sin."*

DOUBTING Elohim's Word is sin. <u>Romans 14:23</u>, *"And he that doubteth is damned if he eat, because he eateth not of faith: for whatsoever is not of faith is sin"*

UNBELIEF in Elohim's Word is sin. In this area the sin above sins is to harden your heart against the clear witness and leading of the Holy Ghost so as to be unable to believe in Yahoshuah. <u>John 16:8-9,</u> *"And when he is come, he will reprove the world of sin, and of righteousness, and of judgment:Of sin, because they believe not on me;"* (also see **Hebrews 4:11-12**).

ALL UNRIGHTEOUSNESS or Un-Messiah-like acts or behavior are sin. <u>1 John 5:17</u>, *"All unrighteousness is sin: and there is a sin not unto death."*

The spectrum of sin

Sin therefore covers a large spectrum of activities, and it is from these that we must **REPENT**. There are however two basic categories of sin.

Inherited sin that all DNA that human kind received from their forefather Adam, which gives us a tendency and disposition to commit acts of sin (a sin nature).

Sin as a choice is the specific acts of wrongdoing which we choose ignorantly or willfully to commit or otherwise take action that is against the interest of God or others.

Even Christians can and do at times fall into the second category of sin (hopefully without making it a habit to commit the same sins) and need to repent when this happens, but the first category (the sin nature) is forever settled by the born again experience.

1 John 1:7-9, *"But if we walk in the light, as he is in the light, we have fellowship one with another, and the blood of Jesus Christ his Son cleanseth us from all sin. If we say that we have no sin, we deceive ourselves, and the truth is not in us. If we confess our sins, he is faithful and just to forgive us our sins, and to cleanse us from all unrighteousness."* (also read **John 3:3-5**).

It is important for us to understand that the answer to sin whether through nature or choice is to repent and forsake it. **Proverbs 28:13**, *"He that covereth his sins shall not prosper: but whoso confesseth and forsaketh them shall have mercy."*

Repentance from dead works
requires a TWO part explanation of :-

(1)   Repentance
(2)   Dead works

To repent, means more than a change of mind, it also means to turn your back on sin, forsaking it, e.g. If you were driving North and repented, you would change your mind and turn the car around and head South.

Repentance could then be described as an inward decision leading to an outward demonstration of that decision. It involves death to selfishness and surrender of self-will to Elohim. **Galatians 5:24**, *"And they that are Christ's have crucified the flesh with the affections and lusts."* (also see **Romans 6:6-13**).

Death is often violent and involves a struggle. It also involves blood, (**Hebrews 2:10-15, Romans 10:12-13, 1 John 1:7-9, Revelations 1:5**). So it is when we decide to follow Yahoshuah and put our old nature to death there is often a violent struggle within, but the death of the flesh nature

49

is sure if we continue to crucify it and die to the World daily. With the death of the old nature we must be sure to replace the old negative habits-patterns with new and positive ones from the Word of Elohim in order to live a repentant life (the opposite of what we used to be).

Repentance may involve restitution of stolen goods, or damaged things like relationships, **Acts 24:16**, *"And herein do I exercise myself, to have always a conscience void to offence toward God, and toward men"*.

This becomes a covenant (contract) between the person repenting and Yah Elohim. If this was an exercise in accounting, we would reconcile regularly our accounts in order to keep our accounting work short.

In the same way, we can live a life where we regularly check-in with Elohim how our current account is and always keep it in balance and in good standing so that we can quickly settle anything that we find is a debt owed or outstanding.

Finally, repentance means forsaking sin (see **Acts 19:13-20**). It is the Bible preparation and basis for baptism in the name of our Yah Yahoshuah Messiah **Acts 2:38,** *"Then Peter said unto them, Repent, and be baptized every one of you in the name of Jesus Christ for the remission of sins, and ye shall receive the gift of the Holy Ghost"*.

We may further define repentance as the grace of God applied to our lives by the power of personal decision causing us to change the way we think, feel and act concerning that which God has called Sin.

Repentance involves turning from a life that leads us away from God, to a life that leads us towards God. It is a turning from any word, thought or deed that would lead us away from God, to words, thoughts and deeds that lead us towards a better relationship with God.

As said before, at the heart of the word repentance is the idea of **CHANGE**. There cannot be true repentance without change as change is the evidence of repentance.

Repentance is a function of the will not feelings, so when someone decides to repent, they will stop doing wrong and start doing right whether they feel like it or not. In other words they have changed direction in their behaviour and turned 180 degrees e.g. if one stole before repenting, one will stop stealing and start restoring what was stolen once repentant.

Further to it, true repentance implies a Godly sorrow that leads to a total change (see **2 Corinthians 7:8-11**). You must be truly sorry for sin, sorry enough to do something about putting it right.

Repentance is not:-

- Regret or rethinking

- Remorse (feeling sorry for yourself or your sin).

- Self-condemnation

- Shame

- Resolution or problem-solving

- Fear

True repentance, as offered in the Bible requires a change both in attitude and action **Matthew 3:8**, *"Bring forth therefore fruits meet for repentance:"* (also **Acts 26:20**).

Repentance is a condition for pardon and forgiveness by Elohim, but it is not a work someone does to earn the right for pardon, forgiveness is not an entitlement but a privilege to receive from Yah

Acts 3:19, *"Repent ye therefore, and be converted, that your sins may be blotted out, when the times of refreshing shall come from the presence of the Lord."* (also check **Isaiah 55:7**).

Repentance is the primary condition before a candidate can be Born-again (Acts 2:38).

It is the way given by Elohim for Christians to maintain a pure relationship with him whenever we commit a specific act of sin.

The way to correct sin is to go to Elohim in prayer quickly and repent (1 John 1:9, Isaiah 1:16-18, Psalm 19:12-13).

When a person truly repents, it brings results in their lives that others can see and bear witness to. The Bible calls this the fruit of repentance **(Luke 3:8-14).** <u>Luke 15:10</u>, *"Likewise, I say unto you, there is joy in the presence of the angels of God over one sinner that repenteth."*

The necessity of repentance

The Bible places more importance on repentance than some of us think, the word "repent" in its various forms is mentioned some 110 times in the Bible. After keeping silent for 400 years Elohim's first words by His Prophet (John Baptist) were repent.

Yahoshuah began His ministry with the same message and later on, the Apostles and Disciples were given the same message again – (**Matthew 3:2, Matthew 4:17, Acts 2:38**).

An excellent illustration of repentance is to be found in **Matthew 21:28-32** – In the parable of the two sons. One said he would obey and didn't, the other son said that he couldn't obey and did

53

the right thing. The one that obeyed is the one that pleased the Father because he repented and still did the right thing.

Dead works are actions that lead to death, in other words SIN. **Romans 6:23**, *"For the wages of sin is death; but the gift of God is eternal life through Jesus Christ our Lord."*

Dead works occur when we act on thoughts Elohim never gave us; when we do that which God never called us to do, but which we have decided out of our own imagination.

Dead works occur when we are either motivated by self e.g. the Prodigal son, or duty - like his elder brother (sense of duty without love produces dead work).

WHAT SHOULD WE REPENT FROM? (Here are a few practical examples.)

WICKED WAYS	2 Chronicles 7:14
WORLDLINESS	1 John 2:-17
SATANIC INVOLVEMENT	Acts 26:18
IDOLATRY	1 John 5:21
LUKEWARMNESS	Revelations 3:15, 16, 19
LACK OF LOVE	Revelations 2:4, 5

Back to the two types of dead works

A)   The works of the flesh

B)   The works of the Law

The works of the flesh are characterized by the word, "Self" - Self-indulgence, selfishness, self-gratification, everything to do with looking out for number-one is flesh based. The key letter is "I". A list of the sins connected with this form of dead works is found in

Galatians 5:19-21, *"Now the works of the flesh are manifest, which are these; Adultery, fornication, uncleanness, lasciviousness, Idolatry, witchcraft, hatred, variance, emulations, wrath, strife, seditions, heresies, Envyings, murders, drunkenness, revellings, and such like: of the which I tell you before, as I have also told you in time past, that they which do such things shall not inherit the kingdom of God."*

The works of the law are characterised by duty and SELF-RIGHTEOUSNESS, self-justification and trying to buy Elohim's favour by some form of self-effort. This type of dead work involves a great deal of inhibition of sin by legislation (use of the law or rules to control sin).

Best illustrations of this lesson are:-

LUKE 10, The story of Martha and Mary. Martha was busy trying to get approval through what she did.

Luke 15, The story of the Prodigal son and his elder brother. The prodigal was very selfish and wanted personal gratification. His older brother however, was self-righteous and was once again working for approval.

Luke 3:4-14, Speaks of bringing forth fruits worthy of repentance ultimately evidence that proves a change has taken place.

Ezekiel 18:20-32, Deals with turning from sin to live. Each of us must turn from sin for our personal benefit. Repentance only benefits the person who repents.

The results of repentance

Elohim's Word is clear about true repentance. Whether a Saint of Elohim or a sinner in need of salvation, the only way to get results from Elohim when in sin, is to sincerely repent and break off your sins by repenting and showing mercy to the poor .

<u>Daniel 4:27</u>, *"Wherefore, O king, let my counsel be acceptable unto thee, and break off thy sins by righteousness, and thine iniquities by shewing mercy to the poor; if it may be a lengthening of thy tranquillity."* The result is that Elohim forgives us.

1. Elohim for Messiah's sake forgives you, **Ephesians 4:32.**
2. All trespasses repented of are forgiven, **Colossians 2:13.**
3. We have the forgiveness of sins, **Colossians 1:14.**

Seven works of repentance

Along with simultaneous events of other kinds, the following seven things happen when a person is truly repentant (**2 Corinthians 7:9-11**).

1. Diligence - A watchfulness lest there is a recurrence of the sin developing.

2. A clearing away of guilt by restitution.

3. A feeling of indignation or hatred of sin develops.

4. The sincere fear of Elohim and sin's results in our life.

5. A strong desire to be right with and obedient to Elohim's Word.

6. Zeal in the work of Yah and His cause.

7. Revenge in the sense of being honest and just with yourself and hard on the devil.

Repentance for the saved

After being born again there are times of failure and sin in the life of every Christian. This is not Elohim's plan for the Christian yet in his mercy it is something He made provision for to aid us in our decision to go on unto perfection.

We are to deal with sin in this circumstance as we did with the sin problem before salvation, REPENT. We are to be overcomers living above the authority and power of sin and reserved one day to be delivered from its very presence.

Yet in the present we can at times fall short of the ideal because of the weakness of our own human desires, and need to act decisively in order to maintain and continue to build our relationship with Father Elohim. It is quick and sincere repentance that makes our continued fellowship with Father possible.

When we confess our sins He forgives and cleanses us in return (**1 John 1:7-9**).

Confession alone is not enough however, we must also FORSAKE sin to receive mercy, (**Proverbs 28:13**).

We have an advocate with the Father should we sin, (**1 John 2:1-2**).

It is in prayer that we are to ask for forgiveness, (**Matthew 6:5-15**).

Father still forgives both Saint and sinner when they truly repent. Blasphemy against the Holy Ghost or speaking against the clear operation of the Holy Ghost and to so harden our hearts against what Elohim is purposing to accomplish in our life.

To the point where the Holy Ghost is unable to minister to us is the one and only sin Elohim will not forgive.

Each individual should be watchful when speaking about the Holy Ghost and never dare to speak about Elohim's Spirit in a disrespectful manner (**Matthew 12:31-32**).

Summary

a. Repentance is basically — turning from sin, turning to Elohim

b. The word sin means to miss the mark and it is the cause of all the problems in the world around us and what we repent from and of.

c. Not everything is a sin

d. There are two basic categories of sin: Inherited sin and sin that we choose to commit.

e. We repent of dead works of which there are two types: Selfishness (works of the flesh) and self-righteousness (works of duty).

f. It not just the unsaved that need to repent, the saved need to live a life of repentance and keep their account short with Yah.

The search your Bible section

1. What is repentance?

2. Who should repent?

3. By whom is repentance produced and given?

4. How may we know when someone has repented?

5. What is the connection between repentance and restitution?

6. What kind of person must one acknowledge one's self to be in order to repent?

7. What is the result of a lack of repentance?

8. What did the Apostles preach foremost?

9. If you sin what should your first response be?

10. What is the first and second command of the Gospel?

Acts 17:30, 1 John 1:9, Mark 1:5, Matthew 9:13, Luke 13:3, Luke 19:1-10, Acts 5:31, 2 Corinthians 7:8-11, Mark 6:12, Matthew 3:8.

Discussion

1. Which scripture in this lesson stood out most to you?

2. What are your observations about the lives of people who are unwilling to repent?

3. List some things that you believe are fruits of repentance.

4. How did you define repentance before this lesson and how do you define it now. What has changed for you?

5. How can you use the knowledge gained in the lesson to live by?

6. What in this lesson is most important for you?

Chapter Three

PRAYER AND FASTING

Introduction

Prayer is first and foremost communication between man and Elohim. It means talking to Elohim with your voice and letting Him talk to you (**Psalm 5:1-3; Psalm 142:1-2**).

It is thanksgiving, needs and desires being offered up to Elohim in faith that He will answer, keeping the petitions in harmony with the teaching of Elohim's Word concerning what is being prayed about or for.

Prayer is a way of life and not just a part of life. For this reason we need to work our lives around prayer, and not prayer into our lives.

The principles of prayer and fasting - **James 5:16,** *"Confess your faults one to another, and pray one for another, that ye may be healed. The effectual fervent prayer of a righteous man availeth much."*

There are a number of valid reasons why we as Christians aught to pray. The first reason is that prayer is the source of strength and nourishment for all Christians, and without it a Christian's spiritual life dries up after becoming shallow –

Psalm 32:3-7, *"When I kept silence, my bones waxed old through my roaring all the day long. For day and night thy hand was heavy upon me: my moisture is turned into the drought of summer. Selah. I acknowledge my sin unto thee, and mine iniquity have I not hid. I said, I will confess my transgressions unto the Lord; and thou forgavest the iniquity of my sin. Selah.*

For this shall every one that is godly pray unto thee in a time when thou mayest be found: surely in the floods of great waters they shall not come nigh unto him. Thou art my hiding place; thou shalt preserve me from trouble; thou shalt compass me about with songs of deliverance. Selah." (see **Isaiah 40:28-31**).

Without regular prayer Christians become weak, lack direction and their joy disappears, before they then gradually leave Elohim's presence.

Nehemiah 8:10, *"Then he said unto them, Go your way, eat the fat, and drink the sweet, and send portions unto them for whom nothing is prepared: for this day is holy unto our Lord: neither be ye sorry; for the joy of the Lord is your strength."* (see **Psalm 16:11**).

Prayer plays a vital role in protecting us from temptation, and without it our relationship with Elohim breaks down - **Matthew 26:41**, *"Watch and pray, that ye enter not into temptation: the spirit indeed is willing, but the flesh is weak."*

The final reason is very simple - it is a sin for us not to pray, **James 4:17**, *"Therefore to him that knoweth to do good, and doeth it not, to him it is sin."*

Prayer in its broadest sense includes:-

a. **SUPPLICATION** - a request for specific benefits from Elohim.

b. **PRAYER** - to talk or vow to Elohim

c. **INTERCESSION** - address to Elohim for oneself or others.

d. **THANKSGIVING** - speech showing gratitude

How to pray

Different people have their own way to pray, but Yahoshuah told us how we aught to pray. The prayer called the Lord's prayer is not meant for repetition, but is rather a perfect pattern for prayer that when followed develops our ability to pray - **Matthew 6:9-13**, *"After this manner therefore pray ye: Our Father which art in heaven, Hallowed be thy name. Thy kingdom come, Thy will be done in earth, as it is in heaven. Give us this day our daily bread. And forgive us our debts, as we forgive our debtors. And lead us not into temptation, but deliver us from evil: For thine is the kingdom, and the power, and the glory, for ever. Amen."* (also check **Luke 11:1-4**).

PLEASE NOTICE THE ORDER OF PRIORITY OF THE HEAVENLY PATTERN FOR PRAYER.

    a. **Praise/Acknowledgement** - of Elohim's name specifically - you can praise Elohim that Yahoshuah is your righteousness, holiness, peace, ever present Elohim, provider, shepherd, healer, deliverer etc.

    b. **Spiritual things/Kingdom priorities** - pray for Elohim's

    c. **For the kingdom to be established** in your life, your home Church and city. Find out what Elohim has said about these subjects

66

then pray for **Elohim's will** (Word) to come to pass.

d. **Material needs/wants** - Put your needs and the needs of others that you know before Yah. Put the bills, the salvation, the promotion, etc.

e. **Cleansing/protection from evil** - Forgiveness is dependent upon forgiving. Ask for discernment of evil and wisdom and alertness to avoid the traps of the enemy. Put on the Armour of Elohim (see Ephesians 6:10-18).

f. **Praise/Thanksgiving** - Praise him for his kingdom, power and glory. Continue your day in praise and worship continually.

The pattern of prayer guidelines

Below is a prayer guide to take you through the same pattern in a little more depth. Yahoshuah said, could you not tarry one hour? That's about how long it will take you to pray through this outline.

I. **OUR FATHER WHICH ART IN HEAVEN, HALLOWED BE THY NAME**

Picture Calvary and thank Elohim you can call him "Father" by virtue of the blood of Yahoshuah.

Hallow the names of Elohim corresponding with the five benefits in the new covenant, and make your faith declarations.

II.   **THY KINGDOM COME. THY WILL BE DONE.**

Yourself, your family (mate, children, other family members) Your church (pastor, leadership, faithfulness of people, harvest).

Nation (city, state/County, and national political and spiritual leaders, harvest)

III. GIVE US THIS DAY OUR DAILY BREAD

Be in the will of Elohim (prayer life, church, work habits, obedience in giving)

- Believe it is Elohim's will to prosper you.

- Be specific in your requests.

- Be tenacious in your asking.

IV. AND FORGIVE US OUR DEBTS AS WE FORGIVE OUR DEBTORS

- Ask Elohim to forgive you

- Forgive and release others

- Set your will to forgive those who sin against you

V. AND LEAD US NOT INTO TEMPTATION, BUT DELIVER US FROM EVIL

- Put on the whole armor of Elohim (put on the Yah Yahoshuah Messiah)

- Loins girt about with TRUTHFULNESS

- Breastplate of RIGHT LIVING

- Feet shod with PREPARATION to share the Gospel.

- (READINESS) of the gospel of PEACEFULNESS

- Shield of FAITH AND FAITHFULNESS.

- Helmet of SALVATION

- Sword of the Spirit which is the WORD OF ELOHIM in prayer.

- Pray a hedge of protection (you are my refuge, my fortress, my Elohim). Because thou hast made Yah thy habitation. Because He hath set His love upon Me. Because He hath known My name.

VI. FOR THINE IS THE KINGDOM, AND THE POWER, AND THE GLORY FOR EVER

- Make your faith declarations

- Return to praise and remain in an attitude of praise all day long.

Each part of the prayer means something specific. It begins and doesn't actually end but continues with praise. It puts spiritual or kingdom things before material desires.

It involves repentance and forgiveness of sin to keep our relationship with Elohim unbroken. It involves praise and worship that keeps the doors open all the day long to access to His presence.

The Benefits of His name

Benefit	Name	Meaning
SIN FREE	YAH-SIDKENU	"Yah Our Righteousness"
SPIRIT	YAH-MKADDESH	"Yah Who Sanctifies"
SOUNDNESS	YAH-SHALOM	"Yah Is Peace"
PRESENCE	YAH-SHAMMAH	"Yah Is There"
HEALTH	YAH-ROPHE	"Yah Heals"
SUCCESS	YAH-JIREH	"Yah My Provider"
SECURITY	YAH-NISSI	"Yah My Banner"
GUIDANCE	YAH-ROHI	"Yah My Shepherd"

Praying Effectively

Be clear about what Elohim would have you pray about. **Mark 11:24**, *"Therefore I say unto you, What things soever ye desire, when ye pray, believe that ye receive them, and ye shall have them."*

Check your motives for praying about your perceived needs. **Psalm 19:14**, *"Let the words of my mouth, and the meditation of my heart, be acceptable in thy sight, O Lord, my strength, and my redeemer."*

Check whether what you are praying about is in accord with Elohim's word. **Psalm 138:2**, *"I will worship toward thy holy temple, and praise thy name for thy lovingkindness and for thy truth: for thou hast magnified thy word above all thy name."*

Bring Elohim's word to Him and remind Him of what his word says. **Isaiah 55:11**, *"So shall myword be that goeth forth out of my mouth: it shall not return unto me void, but it shall accomplish that which I please, and it shall prosper in the thing whereto I sent it."*

Watch over what you prayed for (**Galatians 4:2**) by continually praising Elohim for answering the request. **1 John 5:13-15** , *"These things have I written unto you that believe on the name of the Son of God; that ye may know that ye have* *eternal life, and that ye may believe on the name of the Son of God. And this is the confidence that we have in him, that, if we ask any thing according to his will, he heareth us: And if we know that he hear us, whatsoever we ask, we know that we have the petitions that we desired of him."*

Elohim has promised instant assurance in His Word but not instant manifestation, so be patient when you have prayed. We do not pray to the office of Elohim as a Son. We pray to the Father in the name of Yahoshuah.

John 16:23-24, *"And in that day ye shall ask me nothing. Verily, verily, I say unto you, Whatsoever ye shall ask the Father in my name, he will give it you. Hitherto have ye asked nothing in my name: ask, and ye shall receive, that your joy may be full."* (also **Colossians 3:17**).

We must pray in faith believing that Elohim hears our prayers and that the answer is ours right now. We must leave the place of prayer with the full assurance of the answer to our prayers before we can see the manifestation of the thing of which we are assured.

Hebrews 11:6, *"But without faith it is impossible to please him: for he that cometh to God must believe that he is, and that he is a rewarder of them that diligently seek him."* (also **see Mark**

11:23-24).

Because it is impossible to stay in the place of intense petitioning continuously without getting stale, Elohim has built into the process, a way to enter His presence, renew our strength, and stay in his presence at rest. Elohim dwells in praise so when we dwell in praise, we dwell in his presence.

Psalm 8:2, *"Out of the mouth of babes and sucklings hast thou ordained strength because of thine enemies, that thou mightest still the enemy and the avenger."* (also read **Psalm 16:11, Psalm 22:3, Nehemiah 8:10**).

Prayer is a far reaching activity enabling us to do what otherwise would be impossible for us to do. Spiritual heights can be scaled through prayer. Be determined to practice, prevail and persevere until you achieve and attain what Elohim has promised.

It must be remembered however that there are hindrances, and it is not until these are known and removed that we are ready to persist and persevere until the answer comes, some hindrances to prayer are:-

Sin - Sinful practices, lack of repentance, being condemnatory, critical or complaining; all these issues can stop the answer.

Isaiah 59:1-2, *"Behold, the Lord's hand is not shortened, that it cannot save; neither his ear heavy, that it cannot hear: But your iniquities have separated between you and your God, and your sins have hid his face from you, that he will not hear."* (read **Psalm 66:18** also)

Unforgiveness - incorrect attitudes hinder us in prayer (**Mark 11:23-26**) **Matthew 18:35**, *"So likewise shall my heavenly Father do also unto you, if ye from your hearts forgive not every one his brother their trespasses."*

Not asking according to the will of Elohim (Word of Elohim **1 John 5:14, 15**), **Romans 8:27** , *"And he that searcheth the hearts knoweth what is the mind of the Spirit, because he maketh intercession for the saints according to the will of God."*

Wavering - Ask in faith not doubting the answer will come. (**James 1:5, 8**) Unbelief - Ignorance or disobedience. **Mark 9:23**, *"Jesus said unto him, If thou canst believe, all things are possible to him that believeth."* (read also **Mark 11:23-26, Hebrews 11:6**).

Not asking at all or asking amiss. James 4:3,*"Ye ask, and receive not, because ye ask amiss, that ye may consume it upon your lusts."* (for more see **Matthew 7:7-8**).

Being disobedient to Elohim's Word. <u>1 John 3:19-22,</u> *"And hereby we know that we are of the truth, and shall assure our hearts before him. For if our heart condemn us, God is greater than our heart, and knoweth all things. Beloved, if our heart condemn us not, then have we confidence toward God. And whatsoever we ask, we receive of him, because we keep his commandments, and do those things that are pleasing in his sight."*

Improper husband/wife relationships. <u>1 Peter 3:7</u>, *"Likewise, ye husbands, dwell with them according to knowledge, giving honour unto the wife, as unto the weaker vessel, and as being heirs together of the grace of life; that your prayers be not hindered."*

Unthankfulness, <u>Philippians 4:6</u>, *"Be careful for nothing; but in every thing by prayer and supplication with thanksgiving let your requests be made known unto God."* (also read **Ephesians 5:4, 20)**

Lack of power with Elohim. <u>Acts 1:8</u>, *"But ye shall receive power, after that the Holy Ghost is come upon you: and ye shall be witnesses unto me both in Jerusalem, and in all Judaea, and in Samaria, and unto the uttermost part of the earth."* (see **Ephesians 3:20, 6:10** for more).

Improper motives, <u>Matthew 6:5-8,</u> *"And when thou prayest, thou shalt not be as the hypocrites are: for they love to pray standing in the* *synagogues and in the corners of the streets, that they may be seen of men. Verily I say unto you, They have their reward. But thou, when thou prayest, enter into thy closet, and when thou hast shut thy door, pray to thy Father which is in secret; and thy Father which seeth in secret shall reward thee openly.* But when ye pray, use not vain repetitions, as the heathen do: for they think that they shall be heard for their much speaking. Be not ye therefore like unto them: for your Father knoweth what things ye have need of, before ye ask him."

Failure to use the name of Yahoshuah, <u>**John 14:12-14**</u>, *"Verily, verily, I say unto you, He that believeth on me, the works that I do shall he do also; and greater works than these shall he do; because I go unto my Father. And whatsoever ye shall ask in my name, that will I do, that the Father may be glorified in the Son. If ye shall ask any thing in my name, I will do it."* (see also **Matthew 28:18**).

Fasting in Faith

The most basic definition of biblical fasting is to abstain from food and/or drink to achieve biblical spiritual objectives. Biblical fasting relates to spiritual matters and is usually practiced when our concern for Elohim's interests become more important than our natural desire to nourish our bodies and where a more intense level of commitment and preparation is required, fasting is not usually practiced in isolation.

It is rather it is practiced in conjunction with prayer. Fasting is usually practiced temporarily and periodically for a predetermined length of time, however many people do fast in a seasonal or programmed way and when inspired under submission to their given authority.

The purpose of fasting is to concentrate our attention on moral and spiritual concerns as a higher priority in our life than fleshly appetites. It necessarily involves self-denial. Self doesn't like it but it is a means to an end.

The end is to bring moral and spiritual renewal with the result being that Elohim is glorified and people are set free from sin and demonic oppression (see Isaiah 58).

Fasting like prayer is a way of life, and no surprise that Satan has tried to blind the eyes of the Church to its importance. It is not a legalistic endeavor, but an expected way of life. Yahoshuah said, "moreover, when you fast..." **Matthew 6:16**.

There is no IF, so He took it for granted that believers would fast. Serious minded believers down the ages have practiced fasting as a means of humbling themselves before Elohim.

The Bible seems to indicate four degrees or levels of fasting. These is the partial fast, the normal fast, the extreme fast, and the supernatural fast.

The first degree of fasting is **the limited fast** in this level of fasting, the person eats some food, but it is limited to a certain type of food and the times they eat. Daniel is an example of a believer that practiced this degree of fasting (**Daniel 1:12, 10:2-3**).

The next fast is **the normal fast**, here the person does not eat, but he does drink the necessary liquids (usually water). This is apparently the degree of fasting Yahoshuah chose during His forty days and forty nights of fasting at the beginning of His ministry.

During this type of fast, He was hungry, but not thirsty, **Matthew 4:2**, *"And when he had fasted forty days and forty nights, he was afterward an hungred."*

A most severe level of fasting recorded in the Bible is **the extreme fast**. In this level a person neither eats nor drinks.

Our example is Esther as she went in before the King **Esther 4:16**, *"Go, gather together all the Jews that are present in Shushan, and fast ye for me, and neither eat nor drink three days, night or day: I also and my maidens will fast likewise; and so will I go in unto the king, which is not*

79

according to the law: and if I perish, I perish."

The fast of Moses represents **a supernatural fast**, this however is not to be copied without explicit direction from Elohim as it is an example of something done supernaturally in the presence of and by the power of Elohim (in normal circumstances the body can only go 3 days without water before damage begins to occur).

A fast may be private or public. While an individual's fast is between the person and Elohim **(Matthew 6:16)** a public fast is between Elohim and the people. this can be a church or even a nation, called to a public fast by their leaders **(Jonah 3:5)**.

As a start, please establish a specific time of fasting on a regular basis, such as a specific day of the week. Begin to fast of a small scale and then extend if for longer periods as your body becomes accustomed to going without food.

If you have a physical problem or take medicine, such as insulin, you should consult with your doctor before attempting to fast.

Fasting should be specific and have an aim, although a regular fast can be for matters of a general nature that concern you. Finally begin, just begin with one day and build from there.

Summary

1. Prayer is first and foremost communication between man and Elohim

2. There are a number of valid reasons why we as Christians aught to pray and there are a number of things that can stop a believer from praying. Be sure you know what will hinder your prayers and eliminate them from your life.

3. Without regular prayer Christians become weak, lack direction and their joy disappears, before they then gradually leave Elohim's presence.

4. Prayer plays a vital role in protecting from harm and from temptation.

5. It is a sin for us not to pray.

6. Praying has a pattern that can be learned

7. There are four basic types of fasting. Fasting must be linked to prayer to become successful.

8. Prayer is not just an activity, it must become a lifestyle.

9. Those who pray will have a growing relationship with Elohim according to the measure of mastery.

10. Prayer should always be in faith

11. Search your Bible section - Fit appropriate questions to appropriate scriptures.

12. If a person asks in faith of God in prayer, what has God in turn promised to do?

13. When you ask anything according to God's will, what does he promise to do?

14. What does the prayer of a righteous person do?

15. When God's word abides in you and you abide in Jesus, what can you do

16. Where should we do most of our praying

17. What kind of person's prayer has the Lord promised to hear

18. When the righteous cry what response does God render

19. How often did David pray

20. When we call on God and he answers, what else will he do? Whom should we pray for first?

Psalm 55:17, 1 Timothy 2:1, Matthew 6:6, James 5:16, Proverbs 15:29, Jeremiah 33:3, Matthew 7:7-8, Psalm 34:17, 1 John 5:14-15, Matthew 15:7

Discussion

1. When it comes to prayer do you find it difficult or easy and why?

2. What do you think about fasting and what experience do you have of doing it?

3. Do you tend to combine prayer and fasting or pursue them as separate activities?

4. How can you practically build yourself up in prayer and fasting?

5. What aspect of this lesson has been of greatest value to you and why?

6. What will you seek to develop first and why?

Chapter Four

FAITH TOWARDS ELOHIM

Memory Verse

Hebrews 11:1, *"Now faith is the substance of things hoped for, the evidence of things not seen."*

Introduction

Faith toward God is the second principle of the doctrine of Christ **Hebrews 6:1**.

Faith and repentance are inseparably linked together — **Acts 20:21, Mark 1:15.** Faith is the foundation of the entire Christian life, unless we have it, we cannot have a relationship with God — **Hebrews 11:6; Romans 1:17.**

The Bible definition for faith is found in Hebrews 11:1 above — The first thing to understand when speaking of faith, is that — "the Word" and "faith" are interchangeable words within the context of the subject of faith and the Bible. An examples of this are *"Man shall not live by bread alone, but by every word that proceedeth out of the mouth of God"* **Matthew 4:4** and again.." The Just shall live by faith" Romans 1:17. Again, *"Through faith we understand that the worlds were framed by the Word of God, "* **Hebrews 11:3**.

It's only through Elohim's Word that we can understand creation, or even our very relationship with Him and all that happens through your faith, because you were not there when it all happened. In fact all human understanding occurs because of their faith (rightly or wrongly given) because everything happens based on exploration and that requires faith.

Another example of this is found in the area of science. Science is supposed to be about observable phenomena, but it's not. Scientists were not there when the supposed first amoeba crawled out of the amniotic soup, yet they believe it happened.

They were not there when supposedly the amoeba became a fish nor the fish a frog, nor yet still the frog a snake or the snake a money or the monkey a man. Yet they believe it happened.

They were not there, they did not see, hear, touch, smell, or taste of the events. Yet they strongly assert that there was such a phenomena as evolution when no one knows for sure it happened by their rule of thumb (observable phenomena).

On the other hand, Elohim states in **Genesis 1:1**, *"In the beginning Elohim created the heavens and the earth"*. He asserts that He was there and did it, making His a personal testimony. Now everyone has a choice, do you believe the scientists that were not there, or Elohim who was?

To believe in evolution is to call Elohim a blatant liar. The two systems are systems of belief, and you know belief is not in the realm of science but the arena of faith. What this means for science is that it is actually a religion, because faith is a part of belief or religion.

In this chapter we will be looking at faith as a characteristic of religious belief in order to explain its development and application to our personal and corporate lives as believers. Without faith, it is absolutely impossible to understand spiritual matters or to relate to Elohim, for faith starts with taking Elohim at His Word.

Hebrews 11:6, *"But without faith it is impossible to please him: for he that cometh to God must believe that he is, and that he is a rewarder of them that diligently seek him"*. Again, **Hebrews 11:3,** *"Through faith we understand that the worlds were framed by the word of God, so that* *things which are seen were not made of things which do appear."* One more scripture that explains this further is, **2 Corinthians 4:18**, *"While we look not at the things which are seen, but at the things which are not seen: for the things which are seen are temporal; but the things which are not seen are eternal."*

What is faith all about?

Faith is about trusting someone's word. If we accept Elohim's word on any topic, then by virtue we exclude all other viewpoints and have faith in His Word. That trust represents faith to accept and obey whatever Elohim's word has to say on any and all subjects.

By submitting to the authority of His Word in every area of our life, "the just (saved) shall live by faith (in His Word). We demonstrate that we trust Him to tell us the truth and accept that He is truthful also.

Faith toward Elohim is faith in Elohim, and faith in Elohim is faith in Elohim's word. So because Elohim and His Word are one and the same, if Elohim's Word were to fail (or if He was to lie to us) Elohim would have failed and His word made null and void also.

However, since love never fails, and Elohim (God) is love; Elohim's Word can never fail and He can never lie. However, men can fail to act on

Elohim's Word (and we often do because we don't believe Him) yet Elohim's Word is still true.

The simplest definition of faith therefore, is "To trust". The words 'faith' and 'trust' are interchangeable and synonymous with one another.

So faith could be defined as, "To trust Elohim by taking Him at His Word and behaving as though all that Elohim says is important and true."

In other words, saying and doing whatever Elohim says we ought to say and do. While being fully persuaded that what He has told us is absolutely true and is always in our best interest, concerning the subject at hand or in question.

We need to understand that faith is not a feeling, but a choice. It is a choice of who we will believe or trust. Whether the Word of Elohim or our feelings, circumstances, environment, other humans or the promises of Elohim.

Therefore to doubt Elohim's word is to doubt Elohim Himself, so the opposite of faith is unbelief, or the act of calling Elohim a liar. That is why a person without faith cannot please God (Elohim) see **Hebrews 11:6.**

Unbelief manifests itself in two main ways, either as disobedience to Elohim's known word, rooted in stubbornness; or as doubt because of ignorance (lack of knowledge). Abraham our example never denied the existence of natural problems or faith challenges such as his age, he simply refused to stagger at the promises of Elohim because of Unbelief.

He was fully persuaded Elohim could and would deliver on His promises to him — **Romans 4:19-21**, *"And being not weak in faith, he considered not his own body now dead, when he was about an hundred years old, neither yet the deadness of Sarah's womb: He staggered not at the promise of God through unbelief; but was strong in faith, giving glory to God; And being fully persuaded that, what he had promised, he was able also to perform."*

Faith as defined by **Hebrews 11:1** and **Hebrews 6:1** comes from a Greek word meaning persuasion, credence, conviction of the truthfulness of Elohim, assurance, confidence, and believing.

This term represents "Faith toward God (Elohim)." A good example would be the faith we have when we plant a seed that it will grow. Having no other evidence but the seed, we plant it being persuaded it will grow. Giving the seed credence of its ability to reproduce.

Being convicted that it will deliver results because of past experience or what we have heard about this type of crop. We are assured those who have told us about this seed know what they are talking about.

We rest assured that what we are expecting of the seed will happen are confident of a crop and continue to believe until we see the seedling pop up through the ground. After that, we don't need any faith, because we can see the results in operation.

Romans 8:24-25, *"For we are saved by hope: but hope that is seen is not hope: for what a man seeth, why doth he yet hope for? But if we hope for that we see not, then do we with patience wait for it."*

The word Faith has a number of meanings

Faith as defined above is different from "The faith" as presented in the scriptures. "The faith" refers to the doctrine or teachings declared by Messiah and established by His apostles.

This term refers to your doctrine and the "act of faith" is about your ability to believe and commit to Elohim's Word - **2 Corinthians 13:5**, *"Examine yourselves, whether ye be in the faith; prove your own selves. Know ye not your own selves, how that Jesus Christ is in you, except ye be reprobates?"*

There is also a difference between belief and faith. For while faith is the outward appearance of what a person says they believe.

Faith is also the outward demonstration of what we truly believe. So if someone says they believe in blue, but choose yellow, what they believe has been demonstrated by their actions.

Belief is all about their internal conviction (which cannot be seen). However their faith is about the choices and accompanying actions that demonstrate and display to all what they really believe.

Matthew 9:20-22, *"And, behold, a woman, which was diseased with an issue of blood twelve years, came behind him, and touched the hem of his garment: For she said within herself, If I may but touch his garment, I shall be whole. But Jesus turned him about, and when he saw her, he said, Daughter, be of good comfort; thy faith hath made thee whole. And the woman was made whole from that hour."*

Faith can be seen! Faith can be explained as the substance, proof, or evidence of what you believe, and so it can only be seen through action. If you have faith a chair will hold you up, you sit on it, and if you believe it's not strong enough you don't sit down because it will fall.

Again, if you don't feel a car is safe, you will not

drive it or get into it. Therefore you can see that belief is the internal conviction you experience because you are persuaded of something, while faith is the action you take that can be seen based on your beliefs. So then, one is internal (belief) while the other is external (faith actions).

FAITH	BELIEF
External	Internal
Action	Conviction
Realisation	Expectation

Belief or conviction without action is called 'dead faith'- **James 2:16-24**, *"And one of you say unto them, Depart in peace, be ye warmed and filled; notwithstanding ye give them not those things which are needful to the body; what doth it profit? Even so faith, if it hath not works, is dead, being alone. Yea, a man may say, Thou hast faith, and I have works: shew me thy faith without thy works, and I will shew thee my faith by my works. Thou believest that there is one God; thou doest well: the devils also believe, and tremble. But wilt thou know, O vain man, that faith without works is dead?*

Was not Abraham our father justified by works, when he had offered Isaac his son upon the altar? Seest thou how faith wrought with his works, and by works was faith made perfect? And the scripture was fulfilled which saith, Abraham believed God, and it was imputed unto him for righteousness: and he was called the Friend of God. Ye see then how that by works a man is justified, and not by faith only"

Faith then is can act! Elohim's Word contains the answer to every problem, but until or unless we act on the answer, it will never become the solution or produce the desired results.

An inward conviction is not enough, belief must be converted to faith by action. Belief is the propelling force that causes you to act out what you are having faith in Elohim for.

Faith is also different from hope, faith is putting our belief to work now, hope is the expectation that something will happen in the future because of the actions you will take in the future. Faith therefore, is the foundation or platform upon which hope is built.

Hope gives faith its purpose while faith gives hope its feet and ultimate fulfilment. Take away a person's hope and they will die because they can expect no future, but it takes faith to keep hope alive, because without faith what we hope for can never come to pass.

Faith demands trusting action, and the basis of faith filled action must be Elohim's word, or else the foundation of our faith will be weak. Our faith is only as strong as the object that it rests on or depends upon and the only worthy object of our faith is Elohim's Word.

The reason why faith is quenched by sin is because sin makes faith weak. Sin stops us from trusting Elohim Word due to our own disobedience.

Sin severs our fellowship with Elohim and without our relationship with Him, we are unable to communicate or relate to Him in trust. Sin ultimately is disobedience to Elohim's Word, which is always based on a lack of trust in Elohim's Word, which in turn makes believing Him impossible.

Thus faith and sin are enemies and cannot inhabit the same space or person at the same time. They are mutually exclusive! One excludes the other. A natural example of this would be oil and water.

They cannot inhabit the same space at the same time. If you pour water on oil, they will separate. If you pour oil in water, they will still separate, because they cannot both mingle in the same space.

The only source of true biblical faith is Elohim's word. Faith comes by hearing Elohim's word on the subject area where we have a need — **Romans 10:17**, *"So then faith cometh by hearing, and hearing by the word of God"*.

This means that as Elohim speaks and you understand, your confidence toward Elohim grows that His ability to perform what He promises is true and your confidence in Him also grows that He is telling you the truth and cannot lie.

As the word is heard, it should always be mixed with faith on our part so as to be of profit to us, **Hebrews 4:2**, *"For unto us was the gospel preached, as well as unto them: but the word preached did not profit them, not being mixed with faith in them that heard it."*

In other words, we must act on what Elohim has told us for it to be of any benefit to us. This hearing (understanding) produces growth and inspires renewed hearing and trust, so that the whole process leads to more growth.

Each of us has been given "a measure of faith" **Romans 12:3**, *"For I say, through the grace given unto me, to every man that is among you, not to think of himself more highly than he ought to think; but to think soberly, according as God hath dealt to every man the measure of faith"*

The faith nature of Elohim in seed form is in everyone initially and will grow as we exercise our faith in the Words of Elohim (God). Whether it comes through His recorded Book, The Bible or spoken directly to our hearts as an inspired Word.

This faith operates out of attitudes based on love; this means we get the best results when our motives are pure and unselfish.

Galatians 5:6, *"For in Jesus Christ neither circumcision availeth any thing, nor uncircumcision; but faith which worketh by love."* In other words, faith operates best in the environment of love or unselfish giving.

How is true faith expressed in the life of a believer? It will be expressed by the positive confessions or statements that come out of our mouth which are in line with the Words of Elohim.

Romans 10:9, *"That if thou shalt confess with thy mouth the Lord Jesus, and shalt believe in thine heart that God hath raised him from the dead, thou shalt be saved."* and **Matthew 12:34**, *"O generation of vipers, how can ye, being evil, speak good things? for out of the abundance of the heart the mouth speaketh."*

And again, **Hebrews 10:23**, *"Let us hold fast the profession of our faith without wavering; (for he is faithful that promised;)"*

Faith is expressed by a life of obedience to the word received from Elohim. That is, both in the printed form (the Bible) and in the "Rhema" (A word spoken to you in your spirit by Elohim). Faith and works then operate together in harmony.

Acts 5:32, *"And we are his witnesses of these things; and so is also the Holy Ghost, whom God hath given to them that obey him."*

Romans 6:17, *"But God be thanked, that ye were the servants of sin, but ye have obeyed from the heart that form of doctrine which was delivered you."* It is always obedience to the Words of Elohim that delivers us, why? Because obedience activates faith by action based on the Word of Elohim.

How do we appropriate/activate faith in specific situations?

First we must Locate the promise in Elohim's word that best fits the need presented – **Philippians 4:19**, *"But my God shall supply all your need according to his riches in glory by Christ Jesus."* And again, **John 5:39**, *"Search the scriptures; for in them ye think ye have eternal life: and they are they which testify of me."*

Next, fulfil the conditions attached to the promise(s) you have found that relate to your need.

Deuteronomy 28:1-2, *"And it shall come to pass, if thou shalt hearken diligently unto the voice of the Lord thy God, to observe and to do all his commandments which I command thee this day, that the Lord thy God will set thee on high above all nations of the earth: And all these blessings* *shall come on thee, and overtake thee, if thou shalt hearken unto the voice of the Lord thy God."* Again, **Psalm 37:5**, *"Commit thy way unto the Lord; trust also in him; and he shall bring it to pass."*

Finally, engage the promises in patience, for through them, you accept the trying of your faith and Elohim's testing of your faith by various trials and hardship, such that you grow in faith and continue to serve in obedience to Elohim and benefit by the results of such an exercise of faith to the proportion that it has grown.

Hebrews 6:12-15, *"That ye be not slothful, but followers of them who through faith and patience inherit the promises. For when God made promise to Abraham, because he could swear by no greater, he sware by himself, Saying, Surely blessing I will bless thee, and multiplying I will multiply thee. And so, after he had patiently endured, he obtained the promise."*

What can one do to increase in faith?

Settle it in your heart forever that Elohim's word is true and He cannot lie to you — **Psalm 119:160,** *"Thy word is true from the beginning: and every one of thy righteous judgments endureth for ever."*

Put yourself in the place of hearing the word of Elohim by deliberately listening to the Bible regularly, read it, watch it, meditate on it, be in church to hear it preached, listen to good preaching — **Romans 10:17**, *"So then faith cometh by hearing, and hearing by the word of God."*

Be hearers and doers of the word, once you have heard the word (Elohim has spoken to you, then obey it quickly — **James 1:22**, *"But be ye doers of the word, and not hearers only, deceiving your own selves."*

Exercise the faith that you have, don't worry about what you don't have — **Matthew14:25-29**, *"And in the fourth watch of the night Jesus went unto them, walking on the sea. And when the disciples saw him walking on the sea, they were troubled, saying, It is a spirit; and they cried out for fear.*

But straightway Jesus spake unto them, saying, Be of good cheer; it is I; be not afraid. And Peter answered him and said, Lord, if it be thou, bid me come unto thee on the water. And he said, Come. And when Peter was come down out of the ship, he walked on the water, to go to Jesus."

Finally, Put away all natural reasoning and philosophies of man that speak contrary to the clearly revealed Word of Elohim.

Colossians 2:8, *"Beware lest any man spoil you through philosophy and vain deceit, after the* *tradition of men, after the rudiments of the world, and not after Christ."* (see also **1 Timothy 1:4-7**).

Summary

In conclusion: - Faith toward Elohim is simply to trust Elohim, and have confidence in Him and His word.

To believe what Elohim has said, and that His word is true under all circumstances and even intense scrutiny and that what He has promised He will perform.

The process is that Elohim makes a promise, faith believes it, hope anticipates it and patience waits for it. Faith motivates us to act in line with Elohim's Word through obedience.

Because praise accepts the promise as done it celebrates its manifestation before it ever sees it and manifests the promise as though giving birth to it through praise. But praise is simply the companion of faith and not faith itself.

Search the scripture

1. Of what material does the Bible say faith consists? **Hebrews 11:1**

2. According to **Mark 11:24**, what must we do after we pray?

3. For what very important reason can we believe but not receive according to **James 4:2?**

4. **Numbers 23:19** tells us there is something Elohim cannot do, what is it?

5. **Romans 10:17**, says that faith comes when we do something, what is it?

6. All Elohim's promises come with a declaration of what? **2 Corinthians 1:20.**

7. When you ask in faith believing, what can you expect? **Matthew 21:22.**

8. What instrument is by Elohim to deliver you in **Romans 10:10.**

9. What must you hold unto at all costs according to **Hebrews 11:23.**

10. Not everyone gets what they want immediately, some get it when according to **Luke 17:12-14?**

Discussion

1. What have you noticed about faith when it is small? How about when it is great faith?

2. What do you think makes faith so important to the believer's life?

3. How does a person that has faith differ from one that has belief?

4. How could we develop small faith into great faith?

5. What one thing will you use from this lesson?

Chapter Five

THE DOCTRINE OF THE GODHEAD

Introduction

Who is Elohim (God)? Some will argue that it really doesn't matter if we understand Elohim or not. Do we really need to know who He is as long as we believe in Him? After all Elohim is a mystery?

No one can understand who He is or His identity, can they? However, we read in our text the words of Yahoshuah telling us if we don't believe that He is Elohim we will die in our sins.

Understanding Elohim is therefore a Heaven and Hell issue according to **John 8:24-27**, *"I said therefore unto you, that ye shall die in your sins: for if ye believe not that I am he, ye shall die in your sins. Then said they unto him, Who art thou? And Jesus saith unto them, Even the same that I said unto you from the beginning.*

I have many things to say and to judge of you: but he that sent me is true; and I speak to the world those things which I have heard of him. They understood not that he spake to them of the Father".

In fact there is no more important command **Mark 12:29**, *"And Jesus answered him, The first of all the commandments is, Hear, O Israel; The Lord our God is one Lord:"* Believe in one Elohim is the most important of commands. It matters so much that it determines our eternal destiny.

John 17:3, *"And this is life eternal, that they might know thee the only true God, and Jesus Christ, whom thou hast sent."* It is therefore a must to understand who Elohim is and believe in Him with all of our heart, soul, mind and strength.

Principle 1 - We can understand Elohim

Yahoshuah said (above) that if we did not believe He was Elohim, we would die unsaved. This means it is possible for us to know who Yahoshuah is and that we must know who He is in order to be saved. We must also know and understand who Elohim is if we are to serve Him.

Isaiah 43:10, *"Ye are my witnesses, saith the Lord, and my servant whom I have chosen: that ye may know and believe me, and understand that I am he: before me there was no God formed, neither shall there be after me"*

Since we are commanded by Elohim to know His identity and serve Him. Elohim could not reasonably ask us to do something then make it impossible for us to do so.

Further to this, Salvation is rooted in knowing and understanding who Elohim is. So we must both strive to understand who He is as well as expect Him to reveal Himself to us for the purpose of worship and service in His kingdom.

Principle 2 - Elohim's identity is revealed by the Bible and through His Spirit

Romans 1:20, *"For the invisible things of him from the creation of the world are clearly seen, being understood by the things that are made, even his eternal power and Godhead; so that they are without excuse:"* If then the Godhead can be clearly seen, it's not much of a mystery or as incomprehensive as some would have us believe.

Yahoshuah knew it was possible to know who He

was by revelation through the Father. **Matthew 16:13-17**, *"When Jesus came into the coasts of Caesarea Philippi, he asked his disciples, saying, Whom do men say that I the Son of man am? And they said, Some say that thou art John the Baptist: some, Elias; and others, Jeremias, or one of the prophets.*

He saith unto them, But whom say ye that I am? And Simon Peter answered and said, Thou art the Christ, the Son of the living God. And Jesus answered and said unto him, Blessed art thou, Simon Barjona: for flesh and blood hath not revealed it unto thee, but my Father which is in heaven."

In the passage above:

- Who was Yahoshuah talking to? Who did some think Yahoshuah was?

- Who did Peter say He was? Who did Peter get this information from?

- His identity is revealed by His Spirit personally.

John 4:23-24, *"But the hour cometh, and now is, when the true worshippers shall worship the Father in spirit and in truth: for the Father seeketh such to worship him. God is a Spirit: and they that worship him must worship him in spirit and in truth."* Elohim is a Spirit being, and not a

108

man. This is essentially who or what Elohim (God) is.

That Elohim is not a man is confirmed in: **Numbers 23:19**, *"God is not a man, that he should lie; neither the son of man, that he should repent: hath he said, and shall he not do it? or hath he spoken, and shall he not make it good?"*

Because He is a Spirt, a Spirit has not flesh and bones according to **Luke 24:39**, *"Behold my hands and my feet, that it is I myself: handle me, and see; for a spirit hath not flesh and bones, as ye see me have."*

Principle 3 - Elohim has poured out His Spirit.

The out pouring of Elohim's Spirit was not the manifestation of another god, person or spirit, but the Father's essence (what He is) was made available to men as the Holy Ghost.

Joel 2:28, *"And it shall come to pass afterward, that I will pour out my spirit upon all flesh; and your sons and your daughters shall prophesy, your old men shall dream dreams, your young men shall see visions:"* and again **Acts 2:4, 16-17**, *"And they were all filled with the Holy Ghost, and began to speak with other tongues, as the Spirit gave them utterance*; **Verse 16-17** *"But this is that which was spoken by the prophet Joel; And it shall come to pass in the last days,* *saith God, I will pour out of my Spirit upon all flesh:*

And your sons and your daughters shall prophesy, and your young men shall see visions, and your old men shall dream dreams:" Peter explained that the Holy Ghost was indeed the very Spirit of Elohim, poured into the heart of believers on the day of Pentecost.

So there are not 3 spirits of Elohim, but rather there is only one Elohim who is a spirit. There is only one Lord (Yah).

As **Ephesians 4:4-6** says, *"There is one body, and one Spirit, even as ye are called in one hope of your calling; One Lord, one faith, one baptism, One God and Father of all, who is above all, and through all, and in you all."* When Paul asked who the Lord (Yah) was He said "I am Jesus (Yahoshuah)" **Acts 9:5**.

Principle 4 - When it comes to Elohim, one is all you need.

1Timothy 2:5, *"For there is one God, and one mediator between God and men, the man Christ Jesus;"* How many Elohim's are there? There is only one Elohim, **Galatians 3:20**, *"Now a mediator is not a mediator of one, but God is one."* (also see **Deuteronomy 6:4**).

Elohim does not know of any other deities or gods. If He doesn't know of any besides Himself, then there are no more so why do we invent them? **Isaiah 44:8**, *"Fear ye not, neither be afraid: have not I told thee from that time, and have declared it? ye are even my witnesses. Is there a God beside me? yea, there is no God; I know not any."*

Principle 5 - Only one Elohim created us, there was no trinity and there still isn't.

The Bible reveals only one Elohim created us. **Isaiah 44:2,** *"Thus saith the Lord that made thee, and formed thee from the womb, which will help thee; Fear not, O Jacob, my servant; and thou, Jesurun, whom I have chosen."*

Genesis 1:27, *"So God created man in his own image, in the image of God created he him; male and female created he them."* When speaking of Adam and Eve the language is plural but concerning Elohim it is singular for Elohim is one.

Who was Elohim speaking to in **Ephesians 1:11,** *"In whom also we have obtained an inheritance, being predestinated according to the purpose of him who worketh all things after the counsel of his own will:"* In this passage, Elohim counselled with His own will.

Principle 6 - Elohim is absolutely one and is manifested as Yahoshuah (JESUS) to the world.

Let's look at **1John 5:7-8**, *"For there are three that bear record in heaven, the Father, the Word, and the Holy Ghost: and these three are one. And there are three that bear witness in earth, the Spirit, and the water, and the blood: and these three agree in one."* Consider the three that bear record in heaven.

Then compare with the Water, Spirit, and blood which are three different substances and speaking of them, the Bible states that they agree as one. Speaking of the Father, Word and Holy Ghost it says they are one (one and the same) not 3 persons, one.

Not three separate substances, or even essences, but one person. Jesus (Yahoshuah) acknowledged this in **John 10:30** when He said, *"I and my Father are one."* For anyone to get more than one person out of the Godhead is heretical to a Hebrew.

Who do you see when you see Yahoshuah? **John 14:8-11**, *"Philip saith unto him, Lord, show us the Father, and it sufficeth us. Jesus saith unto him, Have I been so long time with you, and yet hast thou not known me, Philip? he that hath seen me hath seen the Father; and how sayest* *thou then, Show us the Father? Believest thou not that I am in the Father, and the Father in me? the words that I speak unto you I speak not of myself: but the Father that dwelleth in me, he doeth the works. Believe me that I am in the Father, and the Father in me: or else believe me for the very works' sake."*

When you see Yahoshuah, you are looking at the Father in a body. Father is a Spirit, but you can see Him when He is in a body. He was in Yahoshuah for the purpose of reconciling or saving mankind.

2 Corinthians 5:19, *"To wit, that God was in Christ, reconciling the world unto himself, not imputing their trespasses unto them; and hath committed unto us the word of reconciliation."* Our Elohim is able to reconcile and save the human race, because He is dwelling in Yahoshuah. His Spirit indwells or resides in Yahoshuah permanently.

In **John 1:1** , *"In the beginning was the Word, and the Word was with God, and the Word was God."* The Word in this passage was Elohim, not a god, but the very GOD and the only GOD of the universe. The Word = and Elohim = the Word. We can't make Elohim's Word a separate person from Him; no more than your word is another person. You are identified by your thoughts, words, name and personal presence.

Who was the son? **John 1:14**, *"And the Word was made flesh, and dwelt among us, (and we beheld his glory, the glory as of the only begotten of the Father,) full of grace and truth."* According to that passage, the Son is the Word made manifest or physical and the Word is Elohim, thus the one made flesh is Elohim. Elohim in a flesh body is identified as the Son of Elohim.

Who was manifested to the world? **1Timothy 3:16**, *"And without controversy great is the mystery of godliness: God was manifest in the flesh, justified in the Spirit, seen of angels, preached unto the Gentiles, believed on in the world, received up into glory."*

The one manifested to the World of Elohim is though the one we know as Yahoshuah who was manifested as flesh.

Yahoshuah was acknowledge by the Spirit (Father) as His beloved Son in whom He was well pleased. Yahoshuah was seen by angels at His birth and on the cross.

Yahoshuah is preached unto the Gentiles as the Good News of our Yah and Saviour Yahoshuah Messiah. Yahoshuah is believed on in the world as our Saviour and Yahoshuah was received up into glory on the mountain after He had given instructions to His disciples.

If then Elohim - The word was manifested as Yahoshuah Messiah, then it makes perfect sense that Yahoshuah is Elohim.

Principle 7 - Yahoshuah was the one the Bible said He was - Elohim!

Concerning the Godhead **Colossians 2:9-10** in the Bible says, *"For in him dwelleth all the fulness of the Godhead bodily. And ye are complete in him, which is the head of all principality and power:"*

The biblical word that deals with the person of God, is the word Godhead, not the word "trinity" Godhead can be easily explained, whereas the trinity cannot.

That's because Godhead is a biblical word and trinity is a man-made word and a teaching that originates with the Gentiles (in Babylon) and not with the Hebrews. Trinity is not a Word that is found in the Bible, nor is it a teaching of the scripture. So we can say its unbiblical and therefore demonically inspired.

Hebrews have been carried away with this Gentile teaching for far too long. We the Hebrews have always been a monotheistic people and as such cannot accept the teaching of the trinity because we only believe in one Elohim and His name is Yahoshuah.

We believe in one God, and we know His name

and His identity. The apostles never had any problems with believing that Yahoshuah was Elohim, and neither should we.

If there is a controversy today, it is that the, "So called Jews" believe in one God and quote the Shemar (Deuteronomy 6:4) every day. The problem is they do not believe Yahoshuah is the Messiah.

The Christians on the other hand, believe in a trinity and understand that Yahoshuah is the Messiah but do not really believe in one God, but rather a trinity or some other form of godhead.

However, the Spirit in Yahoshuah was Elohim's Spirit, and the flesh (humanity) was called the Son of Elohim. Yahoshuah was both spirit and flesh even as we are tripartite but only conscious of being one, so is He. Just as we are so is He, the real difference is that the Spirit in Him is Elohim's Spirit living out His life as a man.

There is a dual nature (two natures) in Yahoshuah, the nature of a man and the nature of Elohim living as one. As a man He is flesh (fully human) and as Deity He is a fully divine Spirit. So there are two natures and not 2 or 3 persons which would require a different explanation.

The one divine Spirit was Elohim who is called the Father and the flesh was the human that came from Mary's womb called the Son of Elohim

(**1Timothy 2:5**).

Elohim was not a man, but Elohim was in a man (totally different). This is because Elohim is a Spirit and not a flesh human (**Numbers 23:19**). This one Elohim manifested or indwelt the flesh of Yahoshuah Messiah. This is why Yahoshuah is Elohim (**1Timothy 3:16**).

Contrary to common misconception, all religions are not saying the same thing, and all religious paths do not lead to the same place or Elohim. There is but one way to Elohim. <u>**John 14:6**</u> says, *"Jesus saith unto him, I am the way, the truth, and the life: no man cometh unto the Father, but by me."* That is to say, the way He Himself prescribes and reveals is Yahoshuah.

It must be understood that man cannot understand Elohim based on what he sees, imagines or defines Elohim to be; but must do it based on Elohim's personal self-revelation to him.

It is simply not true that all religions are basically the same. Although similar teachings do occur in more than one religion, the differences are marked and vast and for a Hebrew, this teaching of one Elohim coming down to save us is precious, primary and absolutely essential.

What primarily makes many religions into cults is the position which many attribute to Yahoshuah. All over the world various people say different things as to who they believe Yahoshuah was and is; if indeed they believe He ever existed. Yet the Bible is united and clear concerning its declaration of who Yahoshuah is; if we are willing to believe scripture in context and to accept it as the final authority in all matters. So then the question is, who does the Word of Elohim (the Bible) declare Yahoshuah to be?

Apostolic Hebrew Christians will receive some of their greatest opposition from religious circles when they begin to exalt Messiah to His rightful position in the Godhead.

It should be understood and emphasised that the scriptural term applicable when referring to the different revelations of Elohim i.e. (Father, Son and Holy Ghost), is the Godhead and not Trinity or any other man-made term. Godhead means the same as deity. It refers to the state of being Elohim (God), and to the sum total of God's nature.

The Scripture teaches there is but ONE GOD (ELOHIM) and from Genesis to Revelation that is the only number in the Bible ever associated with Elohim. This is because ELOHIM IS ONE.

Many know about Elohim but do not have a personal revelation of the things they read. We all need a revelation of who Elohim is, that is a personal revelation of Elohim (God) Himself. This is something that many of the men of old sought to receive.

1 Peter 1:10-11, *"Of which salvation the prophets have enquired and searched diligently, who prophesied of the grace that should come unto you: Searching what, or what manner of time the Spirit of Christ which was in them did signify, when it testified beforehand the sufferings of Christ, and the glory that should follow."*

IS THE MESSIAH - MAN OR ELOHIM?

MAN	DIETY
A Man of sorrows, **Isaiah 53:3-9**	Your Elohim will come, **Isaiah 35:4-6**
Ploughed upon my back, **Psalm 129:3**	A highway for our Elohim, **Isaiah 40:3**
A Mighty man, **Isaiah 42:13**	From everlasting, **Micah 5:2**
Shame and spitting, **Isaiah 50:6**	The God of the whole earth, **Isaiah 54:5**

The Messiah (Christ) had to have divinity and humanity united in one person, making him both Elohim and man. He was the incarnation of deity in humanity for the purpose of redeeming man, and provided the ultimate union in such a manner that the incarnate One could stand as man's Mediator (**1 Timothy 2:5**).

The incarnate one could not be born by natural generation for the DNA of mankind is corrupted by sin. If the messiah had been born of human generation, He would have been a child of Satan with Elohim dwelling in Him.

So in order to be just to Himself and Just to Satan, Elohim had to ensure that the redeemer would be someone that would be able to pay for man's transgression (human) and be someone over whom Satan had no authority or legal claim against (divine).

Isaiah 9:6, *"For unto us a child is born, unto us a son is given: and the government shall be upon his shoulder: and his name shall be called Wonderful, Counsellor, The mighty God, The everlasting Father, The Prince of Peace."*

And **Isaiah 7:13-14**, *"And he said, Hear ye now, O house of David; Is it a small thing for you to weary men, but will ye weary my God also? Therefore the Lord himself shall give you a sign; Behold, a virgin shall conceive, and bear a son, and shall call his name Immanuel."*

And again, **Matthew 1:23**, " *Behold, a virgin shall be with child, and shall bring forth a son, and they shall call his name Emmanuel, which being interpreted is, God with us.* "

So because sin and death had come upon all men through one man, righteousness and life could also come through one man to all men but this man could not be like all other men who were subject to sin. Elohim would have to go back to the drawing board so to speak and make another Adam.

Romans 5:16-19, *"And not as it was by one that sinned, so is the gift: for the judgment was by one to condemnation, but the free gift is of many offences unto justification. For if by one man's offence death reigned by one; much more they which receive abundance of grace and of the gift of righteousness shall reign in life by one, Jesus Christ.)*

Therefore as by the offence of one judgment came upon all men to condemnation; even so by the righteousness of one the free gift came upon all men unto justification of life. For as by one man's disobedience many were made sinners, so by the obedience of one shall many be made righteous."

The next scripture taken from **1 Corinthians 15:22,** says *"For as in Adam all die, even so in Christ shall all be made alive"*.

The first Adam was formed from the dust of the earth, the rest of the human race were generated by natural processes. However the second Adam was the Lord (Yah) from glory and generated by the Spirit.

1 Corinthians 15:47 *"The first man is of the earth, earthy; the second man is the Lord from heaven."* And following on, **1 Corinthians 2:8** *"Which none of the princes of this world knew: for had they known it, they would not have crucified the Lord of glory."*

What you will see on the next page is a chart that compares, Yahoshuah and Elohim in their reported works and offices. As you read and contrast, you cannot but come to the conclusion that they are one and the same person.

THERE IS ONLY ONE GOD

DEUTERONOMY 6:4 – "Hear O Israel, Yah your Elohim is one Yah"

GOD IS A SPIRIT	Elohim is God	Yahoshuah is God	THERE IS BUT ONE GOD
John 4:23-24 Acts 7:48-49 Acts 17:24-28 Psalm 139:7-12 1 Kings 8:27; Jeremiah 23:230-24	**Elohim is Creator** Genesis 1:1 Genesis 2:7 Job 33:4 Psalm 33:6 Psalm 104:30 Isaiah 40:28 Isaiah 44:24 Isaiah 45:11-18 Malachi 2:10 **Elohim is Redeemer and Saviour** Psalm 78:34-35 Isaiah 47:4 Isaiah 44:6 Isaiah 43:3-11 Isaiah 45:21 Isaiah 49:26 Psalm 106:21 Luke 1:46-47	**Yahoshuah is Creator** Revelations 22:3 Revelations 21:5-7 Revelations 14:6-7 Revelations 10:6 Revelations 4:8-11 Hebrews 1:8-12 Colossians 1:12-17 Ephesians 3:9 1 Corinthians 8:6 John 1:10 **Yahoshuah is Redeemer and Saviour** 1 John 4:14 1 Peter 2:21-24 Acts 20:20 Galatians 3:13 Luke 24:21-29 Luke 2:4-11 John 4:40-42 Philippians 3:20 1 Timothy 1:1-3 1 Timothy 4:10 Titus 1:1-4 Titus 2:10-13 1 Peter 1:10-11 Jude 25	Deuteronomy 6:4-9 Mark 12:28-32 Malachi 2:10 Isaiah 44:6-8 Isaiah 45:2-6, 21-23 Isaiah 46:8-9 I Corinthians 8:4-6 Ephesians 4:5-6 I Timothy 2:5 James 2:19 Revelation 4:2-3
Yahoshuah is Elohim			**Yahoshuah is Man**
Isaiah 7:14 Isaiah 9:6 Micah 5:2 John 1:1, 14 John 1:10 John 8:24, 58-59 John 14:6-11 2 Corinthians 5:19 1Timothy 3:16			Isaiah 7:14 Isaiah 9:6 Luke 1:31; 2:6-7 Acts 17:31 Galatians 4:4 Philippians 2:7-8 1 Timothy 2:5 Hebrews 4:15 Hebrews 7:24-25
	Elohim is the Shepherd Psalm 23 Isaiah 40:10-11 Psalm 100	**Yahoshuah is the Shepherd** John 10:8-12 1 Peter 2:21-25 Hebrews 13:20 1 Peter 5:4	
	Elohim is King Psalm 24 Psalm 44:4 Psalm 74:12 Isaiah 44:10-15 Isaiah 44:6-8 Jeremiah 10:10 Zechariah 14:9	**Yahoshuah is King** Matthew 2:1-6 Luke 19:32-38 Luke 23:3 John 18:37 John 19:21 1 Timothy 6:13-16 Revelations 15:14 Revelations 19:11-16	
	Elohim is the I AM and the I AM He Exodus 3:13-14 Isaiah 43:10-11,25	**Yahoshuah is the I AM and the I AM He** John 18:5-8 Revelations 1:17-18 John 8:24-28	
	Elohim First and Last Isaiah 41:4 Isaiah 43:10-11 Isaiah 44:6,8	**Yahoshuah First and Last** Revelations 1:17-18 Revelations22:13	
	Elohim the Rock Isaiah 17:10-11 Psalm 89:26 Psalm 78:34-35 Psalm 31:3 Psalm 18:2 2 Samuel 22:32 2 Samuel 22:1-3 Deuteronomy 32:1-4	**Yahoshuah the Rock** Matthew 16:17-18 Isaiah 28:16 Acts 4:11-12 1 Corinthians 10:4 Numbers 20:1-11 Ephesians 2:20-22 1 Peter 2:6-8	
	Elohim is coming Psalm 50:1-2 Revelations 19:9, 16 1 Thessalonians 4:13-18 Zechariah 14:4-5	**Yahoshuah is coming** 1 Thessalonians 3:11-13 Matthew 25:31-46 Titus 2:11-13	

123

Yahoshuah is the Lord (Yah) God (Elohim) of the Bible

The names and titles of Elohim describe important aspects of His nature, moral attributes, presence, power and authority. The progressive revelation of the name YHWH or JHWH (The Tetragrammaton) in scripture does not give a complete revelation of Yah Elohim until we see each name being fulfilled in the New Testament.

Jacob sought a fuller revelation, (**Genesis 32:29**) but Elohim did not grant it to him. Manoah, Samson's father asked and again it was not revealed (**Judges 13:18**).

JIREH	PROVIDER	**Heb. 10:10-12**	**Gen. 22:14**
RAPHA	HEALER	**Jam. 5:14,15**	**Ex 15:26**
NISSI	VICTORY	**1Cor 15:57**	**Ex 17:15**
KADESH	SANCTIFIER	**Eph 5:26**	**Ex 31:13**
SHALOM	PEACE	**Jn 14:27**	**Judge 6:24**
SABOATH	LORD OF	**Jam 5:4-7**	**1 Sam 1:3**
ELYON	MOST HIGH	**Luke 1:32,76-78**	**Psalm 7:17**
RAAH	SHEPHERD	**Jn 10:11; Heb.**	**Psalm 23:1**
HOSEENU	MAKER	**Jn 1:3**	**Psalm 95:6**
SIDKENU	RIGHTEOUSN	**1 Cor 1:30**	**Jer 23:6**
SHAMAH	PRESENT	**Matt 28:20**	**Ezek 48:35**

All of these names have their fulfilment in one name – Yahoshuah (also called Jesus) is the fulfilment of all the Old Testament names of Elohim. The highest most exalted name ever to be revealed to man.

<u>Isaiah 52:6</u> , *"Therefore my people shall know my name: therefore they shall know in that day that I am he that doth speak: behold, it is I."* Elohim purposed that His people would know His name. Yahoshuah is that one name.

According to **Zechariah 14:9,** *"And the Lord shall be king over all the earth: in that day shall there be one Lord, and his name one."* As it encompasses and includes all the other names of Elohim within its meaning.

Yahoshuah is the revealed name of Elohim in the New Testament age. It means YHWH IS SAVIOUR (or Yah has become our salvation) and represents the salvation, power, work, presence, and authority of Elohim – (Read **Isaiah 7:14, Matthew 1:23, Luke 2:11; Isaiah 9:6, 1Timothy 3:16**).

It is because this very name is representative of Elohim and of (Yahoshuah) the name that it is the Highest name of all, **Philippians 2:9-10**, *"Wherefore God also hath highly exalted him, and given him a name which is above every name: That at the name of Jesus every knee should bow, of things in heaven, and things in earth, and things under the earth;"*

That is also why no other name can save your soul, **Acts 4:10-12**, *"Be it known unto you all, and to all the people of Israel, that by the name of Jesus Christ of Nazareth, whom ye crucified, whom God raised from the dead, even by him doth this man stand here before you whole.*

This is the stone which was set at nought of you builders, which is become the head of the corner. Neither is there salvation in any other: for there is none other name under heaven given among men, whereby we must be saved." This is also why we must do all, whether word or deed in the name of Yahoshuah –

Colossians 3:17, *"And whatsoever ye do in word or deed, do all in the name of the Lord Jesus, giving thanks to God and the Father by him."* (This means prayer, healings, teaching, preaching, and baptism should all be in the name of Yahoshuah).

Father, Son and Holy Ghost simply describes the offices of the One Elohim, so the reference in **Matthew 28:19,** *"Go ye therefore, and teach all nations, baptizing them in the name of the Father, and of the Son, and of the Holy Ghost:"* This scripture asked you to do baptism in, "the name" so while it describes the scope or offices of the one named Elohim it hints to baptism in one name, "singular" and this is further clarified.

In **Acts 2:38**, *"Then Peter said unto them, Repent, and be baptized every one of you in the name of Jesus Christ for the remission of sins, and ye shall receive the gift of the Holy Ghost."* It tells us what the saving name is and how to apply it to our lives in salvation. Quite simply, Yahoshuah is the name of Elohim.

Objections answered

Many seeming objections can be voiced by the enemy to tempt those whose hearts the Lord (Yah) has opened to have a love for the truth. It is therefore necessary to examine the commonest objections in order that the faithful may not be tempted to doubt on this account.

Most of these seemingly important objections actually occur because of a wrong division of the Word of truth (dealt with already in chapter 1) together with misapplication of supposedly difficult texts.

Getting them into their correct setting, and new beauty and light will radiate from these scriptures into your heart. The main trouble with this question of objections is a certain perverse determination on the part of some people to confuse the scriptures which concern Yahoshuah's Godhead as the Father (a spiritual being), with those which concern His mediator-ship as the Son (a human being).

Yahoshuah is YHWH (The name of Elohim). Its attributes ascribed to Elohim in the Old Testament, are also used in reference to Yahoshuah in the New Testament, demonstrating that Jesus is Elohim. "There is only ONE GOD"

I Corinthians 8:6 says, "But to us there is but one God, the Father, of whom are all things, and we in him; and one Lord Jesus Christ, by whom are all things, and we by him."

The main thing to recognise here again is that Elohim said He would not share his glory with another and that there is no one like or equal to our Elohim - **Isaiah 42:8**, "I am the Lord: that is my name: and my glory will I not give to another, neither my praise to graven images."

And **Isaiah 48:11**, "For mine own sake, even for mine own sake, will I do it: for how should my name be polluted? and I will not give my glory unto another." Last but not least is **Isaiah 40:25**, "To whom then will ye liken me, or shall I be equal? saith the Holy One."

My reasoning is quite simple, since no one can be equal to Elohim, nor like unto Him, if we see someone exhibiting the exact qualities and attributes of Elohim then this person must be Elohim. Did not the Jews make the accusation of Yahoshuah that He made Himself equal to God (Elohim)?

In **John 5:18, we read,** *"Therefore the Jews sought the more to kill him, because he not only had broken the sabbath, but said also that God was his Father, making himself equal with God"*

Did He not make the claim Himself in **John 8:58**, *"Jesus said unto them, Verily, verily, I say unto you, Before Abraham was, I am."* and does not the scripture say of Him "He thought it not robbery to be equal with God."

Philippians 2:6. Yet there is none like our Elohim according to **1 Chronicles 17:20** *"O Lord, there is none like thee, neither is there any God beside thee, according to all that we have heard with our ears."*

Scripture is very clear, Yahoshuah Messiah was fully Elohim (God) and at the same time fully man. Any deviation from this position is not only unscriptural, it is heretical.

Those who attempt to make Yahoshuah something less than Elohim cannot go to the Bible for their justification. Therefore anyone that takes the Bible seriously, must conclude that Yahoshuah of Nazareth was Elohim (God) in human flesh form.

Scripture foretold that Elohim would come as a man, **Isaiah 42:12-13**, *"Let them give glory unto the Lord, and declare his praise in the islands. The Lord shall go forth as a mighty man, he shall stir up jealousy like a man of war: he shall cry,* *yea, roar; he shall prevail against his enemies."*

That He would save and that he would be born is written many thousands of years before it happened. **Isaiah 35:4-6**, *"Say to them that are of a fearful heart, Be strong, fear not: behold, your God will come with vengeance, even God with a recompence; he will come and save you.*

Then the eyes of the blind shall be opened, and the ears of the deaf shall be unstopped. Then shall the lame man leap as an hart, and the tongue of the dumb sing: for in the wilderness shall waters break out, and streams in the desert." And again (**Isaiah 9:6**) and **Luke 2:11**, *"For unto you is born this day in the city of David a Saviour, which is Christ the Lord."*

The Word which was Elohim, He became flesh and made His home among us and we beheld the glory of Elohim. When Elohim became a man through the incarnation, He became man for eternity.

He did not assume humanity as a garment to be worn for thirty-three years and then cast it off to be laid aside, but He became man to be a man forever.

Today, there is a man in heaven sitting in the throne of Elohim as Lord (Yah) and Elohim as a result of the incarnation. **1Timothy 2:5; Revelations 21:5-6; Revelations 1:8, 17,18.**

Since Yahoshuah is BOTH Elohim and man He possesses a total, complete and entire human nature including body, soul and spirit.

As Elohim He has all the power and authority of deity. When Yahoshuah refers to His Father, it is the flesh acknowledging the Spirit is greater than His humanity (Holy Ghost, or Deity) that which begat Him.

When Yahoshuah prays it is not one divine person praying to another divine person; it is the flesh (humanity) praying to Deity or Spirit (God).

It must be understood clearly that FLESH and SPIRIT exist simultaneously in the person of Yahoshuah Messiah (Christ).

Distinguishing between Deity and Humanity are crucial to understanding the Godhead. You cannot make flesh into spirit, and neither can you make spirit turn into flesh (**John 1:1,14**).

It is the flesh (Humanity) that contains or houses the Spirit of Elohim (Deity), and it is that Spirit of Elohim (deity) that Manifests itself or works through the flesh (Humanity).

Yahoshuah is fully Elohim and not just an anointed man, yet He is fully man and not just the appearance of man. Yahoshuah is at the same time fully man and fully Elohim (**2 Corinthians 5:19; Colossians 2:9**).

When Yahoshuah speaks or is spoken of in scripture we should seek to determine whether it is with reference to His Deity or His Humanity. We should therefore not think of 2 Gods or persons, but rather spirit (deity) and flesh (humanity).

Yahoshuah was human

Although he was supernaturally conceived by the Holy Spirit, Yahoshuah Messiah, Elohim in human flesh, was also fully man and the scriptures are definite concerning His humanity.

* He grew intellectually and physically **Luke 2:52.**

   He desired food,   **Matthew 4:2.**
* He became tired,   **John 4:6.**
* He needed sleep,   **Matthew 8:24.**
* He cried   **John 11:35.**
 * He died,   **John 11:33.**

Therefore, it is made plain by scripture that Yahoshuah was genuinely human. He possessed all the attributes of humanity without exception and had to be human in order to qualify to rescue man from sin.

However, He also had to be Elohim in order to be able to have the power and authority to enforce the outcome of the incarnation, can you imagine Satan being fair or truthfully accepting the outcome that we now enjoy unless the one who conquered him is greater in authority than he is?

Yahoshuah was Elohim

Yahoshuah of Nazareth was a man but He was more than just a man. He was Elohim in human flesh. While scripture teaches He was a man, they likewise make it clear that He was Elohim.

- He was equal to Elohim, **John 5:18; 10:33.**

- He created all things, **John 1:3; Colossians 1:6.**

- He offered forgiveness of sins, **Mark 2:5-12**

- He accepted worship, **Matthew 2:2,11; Matthew 28:9,17; John 9:38.**

LET US MAKE MAN, <u>Genesis 1:26-27</u>, *"And God said, Let us make man in our image, after our likeness: and let them have dominion over the fish of the sea, and over the fowl of the air, and over the cattle, and over all the earth, and over every creeping thing that creepeth upon the earth. So God created man in his own image, in the image of God created he him; male and female created he them."* and again THE MAN IS BECOME AS ONE OF US,

<u>Genesis 3:22-24</u>, *"And the Lord God said, Behold, the man is become as one of us, to know good and evil: and now, lest he put forth his hand, and take also of the tree of life, and eat, and live for ever: Therefore the Lord God sent*

him forth from the garden of Eden, to till the ground from whence he was taken. So he drove out the man; and he placed at the east of the garden of Eden Cherubims, and a flaming sword which turned every way, to keep the way of the tree of life."

In **Genesis 1:27** we find out that Elohim made man in "His" image. Nothing plural about that, is there?

In **Genesis 3:24** we find that "He" drove out the man. If Elohim in His absolute essence is a plurality of persons, why am I who am made in the image of Elohim, NOT a plurality of persons? I am threefold: spirit, soul, and body, but only ONE person.

Elohim has a plurality of attributes, such as power, holiness, knowledge of Good and evil, love, light, etc. (Also see **Job 38:4-7** it explains who the "us" was).

THE RIGHT HAND OF GOD, <u>Acts 7:55-56</u>, *"But he, being full of the Holy Ghost, looked up stedfastly into heaven, and saw the glory of God, and Jesus standing on the right hand of God, And said, Behold, I see the heavens opened, and the Son of man standing on the right hand of God"* (see **Romans 8:34; Ephesians 1:20; Colossians 3:1**).

As Elohim is a Spirit who cannot be seen and is everywhere present. As a Spirit He does not have a right hand or a left. What the right hand signifies is the favour of Elohim which can be seen in the following passage (**Psalm 77:7-10**).

Look at **Luke 11:20**, *"But if I with the finger of God cast out devils, no doubt the kingdom of God is come upon you."* This clearly shows that the finger and hand of God are expressions symbolic of His power. It means the place of power, favour, acceptability, and authority.

THERE ARE THREE THAT BEAR RECORD 1 John 5:7, *"For there are three that bear record in heaven, the Father, the Word, and the Holy Ghost: and these three are one."* The Father, the Word and the Holy Ghost are everywhere present. These are NOT THREE INDIVIDUAL PERSONS.

"THESE THREE ARE ONE (SPIRIT)" present everywhere at the same time. **2 Corinthians 3:16-17**, *"Nevertheless when it shall turn to the Lord, the vail shall be taken away. Now the Lord is that Spirit: and where the Spirit of the Lord is, there is liberty."* In **Ephesians 4:4-7** we learn, there is but one Spirit of Elohim, and Elohim is that Spirit, (**John 4:24**).

IS MARY THE MOTHER OF GOD? No! Mary was a fallen creature of the line of Adam. She had 7 children, 4 boys and 3 girls. Apart from being chosen by the Lord (Yah) for a special work she was no different than your mother or mine. She needed salvation even as we, and received the Holy Ghost the same way we do, (**Acts 1:14-15; 2:4**).

MY FATHER IS GREATER THAN I, John 14:28, *"Ye have heard how I said unto you, I go away, and come again unto you. If ye loved me, ye would rejoice, because I said, I go unto the Father: for my Father is greater than I."*

Yes the omnipresent spirit of Elohim is greater or higher in nature than that flesh man. Only as a man is the Son (flesh) inferior to His Father (spirit). It is therefore error to worship the Father as a separate person from His Son (body or flesh). Yahoshuah has all power in heaven and earth. The very Elohim dwelling in Messiah makes Him very Elohim, yet it will do us well to remember that Divinity is greater than humanity.

DID ELOHIM DIE ON THE CROSS? No! Elohim's body did. Remember Elohim is a Spirit. It is accurate to say that Elohim (in Christ) suffered in the flesh, **1 Peter 4:1**; Elohim (the Word) in the flesh of His son, died, **1 Peter 3:18**.

Elohim did not send someone else to the cross. Elohim gave Himself, in person but only His body could be killed, (**Titus 2:13; Acts 20:28**). Jesus said, *"Destroy this temple (body) and in three days I will raise it up."* **John 2:19**.

The Elohim part of Jesus could not die, but the Son did die. It was not a natural death. It was deity withdrawing from humanity on that day and on that cross.

WHO DID JESUS PRAY TO, Himself? No! When He prayed it was an example of flesh (man) praying to Deity (spirit) <u>Psalm 65:2</u>, *"O thou that hearest prayer, unto thee shall all flesh come."*

What does the term **ONLY BEGOTTEN Son of Elohim** mean? **John 3:16**. It means that Elohim has no other son that is begotten - born or specially created - of a woman but Yahoshuah.

Yahoshuah Messiah is the only off-spring of Elohim through the process of conception, development, and physical birth.

SON OF GOD OR GOD THE SON? The Bible never calls Yahoshuah, "God the Son" neither is Mary called the Mother of God (Elohim).

Yahoshuah is Elohim (God), and in His incarnation He is called the SON OF GOD for in Him dwells ALL the fullness of the Godhead bodily (**Colossians 2:9**). These other terms are simply unscriptural.

GOD IN THREE PERSONS - Scripture leaves us in no doubt that there is only one person in the Godhead. Spirit is not a person, as it doesn't have flesh and blood.

No man directly can see the invisible Spirt of Elohim. Thus the only person you can see is Yahoshuah (**Exodus 33:20; 1 John 4:12; John 1:18; 1 Timothy 3:16, Colossians 2:9**).

SUMMARY

The question non Hebrew-apostolics need to answer is this:-

Is Yahoshuah in the Godhead or is the Godhead (deity) in Yahoshuah. **Colossian 2:9** says, *"The fullness of the Godhead is in Yahoshuah."* Yahoshuah is Elohim, not part of Elohim or 1/3 of Elohim. It's all in Him and He is all Elohim. Yahoshuah Messiah is Elohim (God).

Today some cannot find the true God (Elohim). This is because the flesh body of the Son acted as a veil for the Yah (Lord) Elohim (God the Father). The veil of His flesh has hidden the one true Elohim from many Christians, **2 Corinthians 3:16-17.** The Jew, the Moslems and Jehovah Witnesses deny that YHWH of the Old Testament dwells in Mary's son. Why because they can't see it.

2 Corinthians 4:3-4. Because unbelievers have been blinded to the truth.

The Jews know that the Messiah is and will be the person of God but they don't believe that Yahoshuah is the Messiah. Christians know that

Jesus is the Messiah, but many do not believe that He is the very single and only person of Elohim.

Elohim came in the flesh and was a snare (trap) to catch the Jews in their unbelief. YHWH veiled in flesh, is a stone of stumbling and a rock of offense to all who deny His Deity (**Isaiah 8:14,15; Romans 9:32,33; 1 Peter 2:6-8**).

Believing upon Elohim biblically upholds Christian belief in at least three ways:-

It restores biblical terminology, and thought patterns from a distorted view of Elohim and clearly establishes New Testament Christians as the spiritual heirs of Old Testament Judaism.

It upholds and reveals the true identity and absolute deity of the Yah (Lord) Yahoshuah (Jesus) Messiah (Christ) **1 Timothy 3:16**.

It places proper biblical emphasis on the name of Yahoshuah thus making the power of the name available to every believer and restoring biblical salvation with Hebrew Apostolic power.

Finally I close by saying, Elohim is one, His name is one, and there is no other name than Yahoshuah which can save you, heal you, answer your prayers, cast out devils or bless your food. Whatever you do in word or deed do all in the name of Yahoshuah (Jesus) **Colossians 3:17**.

Remember all means "all". For there is no other name given under heaven among men by God which can save you from your sins (**Acts 10:12**).

In the final analysis you may have been taught by sincere people, yet even sincere people can be sincerely wrong. Whichever way things go, we aught to believe and obey God rather than men **Acts 5:29**.

What should you do?

1. Believe in One absolute Elohim manifested in many ways and reject the man made idea of a trinity.

2. Believe that Yahoshuah Messiah is Elohim manifested in a flesh body.

3. Believe that salvation comes through repentance, baptism in the name of Yahoshuah and the infilling of Elohim's Spirit.

4. If you have not yet been baptised in the name of Jesus/ Yahoshuah (even if you have been baptised some other way), be baptised in the name of Yahoshuah and be filled with the Holy Spirit as the Bible teaches.

Search the scripture - pair appropriate scripture to the questions

1. Which scripture declares God is His Word in the flesh?

2. Which scripture shows that Jesus (Yahoshuah) is Almighty God in the flesh?

3. How much Godship or Deity is resident in Yahoshuah Messiah?

4. Who was made manifest through the mystery of Godliness?

5. How many Gods does the Almighty declare that there are?

6. Who is our Creator as declared by scripture?

7. What is the meaning of Emmanuel when interpreted?

8. Why was Yahoshuah so called according to the scriptures?

9. Could Yahoshuah be called the everlasting Father?

10. To whom shall every knee bow in eternity?

Colossians 1:16; Matthew 1:21; Colossians 2:9; Isaiah 45:21-23 and Philippians 2:9-10; John1:1,14; Isaiah 9:6; Revelations 1:8; Deuteronomy 6:4; Matthew 1:23; 1 Timothy 3:16.

Discussion

1. When it comes to the Godhead, what do you think is the most popular form of belief among modern Christians?

2. What d999oes the Godhead mean to you?

3. What did you first think about this subject before the Chapter began and have you moved from that understanding?

4. Compare oneness with trinity and what are your thoughts?

5. How will you use the information that you have been given to help others?

6. What is it that you feel stands out for you in this lesson?

Chapter Six

THE DOCTRINE OF BAPTISMS

Introduction

After we have repented from our dead works and started exercising faith in God, we then need to go on to good works. The first good work we need to do is baptism.

To begin with, we see that we have an apparent contradiction in the study of the doctrine of baptisms **Hebrew 6:2** – says "baptisms" and the good work is "baptism". Before I explain what is going on, let's take a look at the various baptisms the Bible mentions. You may be surprised at the number of them!

1. Baptism of repentance (or of John)

The baptism which John performed prior to and during the ministry of Yahoshuah. The scripture reference is **Matthew 21:25**, *"The baptism of John, whence was it? from heaven, or of men? And they reasoned with themselves, saying, If we shall say, From heaven; he will say unto us, Why did ye not then believe him?"* This baptism was superseded and replaced by:

2. Baptism in the name of the Lord (Yah) Yahoshuah

After Yahoshuah's resurrection, this is how the apostles baptised. The ceremony appears to have been the same, but the authority of the ones administering it had changed, i.e. from John to the messengers of Yahoshuah. *"And he said unto them, Unto what then were ye baptized? And they said, Unto Johns's baptism.*

Then said Paul, John verily baptized with the baptism of repentance, saying unto the people, that they should believe on him which should come after him, that is, on Christ Jesus. When they heard this, they were baptized in the name of the Lord Jesus." **Acts 19:3-5**.

3. Baptism of the Holy Ghost

This is John the Baptist speaking: *"I indeed baptize you with water unto repentance: but he that cometh after me is mightier than I, whose shoes I am not worthy to bear: he shall baptize you with the Holy Ghost and with, fire:"* **Matthew 3:11**. We will go into more detail later.

4. Baptism of fire

Using the same scripture as above, we note that the conjunction "and" denotes two separate things going on - the baptism of the Holy Ghost and the baptism of fire. The baptism of fire is a concept that is even well known out in what we call the "worldly" circles. It is a season of intense trial which under the hand of God is used to purify His people.

Some other baptisms that do not directly have a physical application.

- ✓ Baptism into Christ and His death
- ✓ Baptism unto Moses
- ✓ Baptism into one body
- ✓ Baptism for the dead

Peter tells us that the Great Flood was symbolic of our baptism. *"..when once the longsuffering of God waited in the days of Noah, while the ark was a preparing, wherein, few, that is, eight souls were saved by water. The like figure whereunto even baptism doth also now save us (not the putting away of the filth of the flesh, but the answer of a good conscience toward God by the resurrection of Jesus Christ"* **1 Peter 3:20-21**.

We also note the recurring theme of how our repentance and subsequent obedience by faith toward God will affect our conscience. It also foreshadows our lesson on resurrection from the dead.

The baptism unto that signifies what happened to Moses and the children of Israel as they passed through the Red Sea, which was a type and shadow of passing from their old life in Egypt to their new life in the promised land.

Baptisms that most apply today

Now after, removing the ones which do not apply, we are left with three baptisms –

1. **The baptism of Jesus or water baptism**

2. **The baptism of the Holy Ghost**

3. **The baptism of fire**

The first two bring into the one body and the third purifies us as member of that same body. This is a nice progression, for it is a person, usually a minister of the gospel, who baptizes us into Yahoshuah.

Then according to the scriptures we read above, it is Yahoshuah who baptizes us in the Holy Ghost and fire. Finally, it is the Holy Ghost (Spirit of Yahoshuah) who baptises us into one body.

So, is it four or is it one? It is one baptism with many aspects. Baptism is not just what we call an "ordinance" or a "sacrament", like a marriage ceremony it is covenantal or contractual.

Certainly there must be the act of being immersed in water. But having a marriage ceremony without living like you are married makes no more sense than a baptismal ceremony without living like you were baptized.

Baptism is not just an act - it is a way of life and it is the way Yahoshuah lived His life. In response to a question some of His disciples asked Jesus responded, *"Are ye able to drink of* the cup that I shall drink of, and to be baptized with the baptism I am baptised with?" **Matthew 20:22**.

Later on, He said, *"But I have a baptism to be baptized with; and how am I straitened till it be accomplished"* **Luke 12:50**. This was after His baptism in the Jordan.

He was speaking of His death on the cross. You will recall that also in the Garden of Gethsemane immediately prior to His crucifixion that He asked the Father to "remove this cup", but "not my will, but Thine be done." He also said, *"And whosoever doth not bear his cross, and come after me, cannot be my disciple."* **Luke 14:27.**

Baptism then is a lifelong adventure of going down in death and rising in resurrection power. *"Know ye not, that so many of us as were baptized into Jesus Christ were baptized into his death? Therefore we are buried with him by baptism unto death: that like as Christ was raised up from the dead by the glory of the Father, even so we also should walk in newness of life."* **Romans 6:3-4**.

When Paul spoke of "The Doctrine of Baptisms", he was referring specifically to: -Water baptism in the name of Jesus Christ (Yahoshuah) and the baptism of the Holy Ghost.

These are the two essential elements outlined in **John 3:1-8**; which are absolutely necessary before one can go on unto perfection. We must first establish or settle these baptisms (Water and Spirit), otherwise known as the born again experience, or the New Birth (a process which begins with repentance and includes the BAPTISMS is made void) **Acts 2:38.**

Yahoshuah introduced it to Nicodemus, and taught that it is essential for everyone to have this experience. He said, "*You must be born again*", **John 3:7**. This was not and is not a suggestion, it is a command.

Yahoshuah taught that there are essentially two requirements to be fulfilled in order for a person to be considered "born again"; they are :- *"Except a man be born of the water and of the Spirit he cannot enter into the Kingdom of God"*, <u>**John 3:5**</u>. He also indicates that there will be a universal sound whenever a person is born of the Spirit, <u>**John 3:8**</u>, *"The wind bloweth where it listeth, and thou hearest the sound thereof, but canst not tell whence it cometh, and whither it goeth: so is every one that is born of the Spirit."*

The word "wind" is also translated as, "spirit".

So the spirit makes a sound wherever it goes and you hear the sound of it. Going back to the original analogy, wind makes sound in the trees and as it passes buildings, but you can't tell the direction its coming from.

The same thing happens with the move of the Spirit. However, everyone that gets filled with the Spirit of Elohim makes a universal sound just like the wind in the trees or around the buildings.

When children are born, there is a universal sound that demonstrates life. When spiritual children are born again, there is also a universal sound and its speaking in tongues according to the Bible and we will demonstrate that later.

This is what is at the heart of the matter. Hence it's on this that we will concentrate our efforts to explaining more in this chapter - **John 3:1-8, Mark 16:16, Acts 2:38.**

Further to this, it is important to focus on the word "CANNOT" in Yahoshuah's statement. We believe that if Yahoshuah says CANNOT, He means CANNOT. Let us look more closely at the birth of the Water.

Part one - Birth of the water

What is baptism? The word BAPTISM comes from a Greek word meaning - to dip, immerge, plunge under, overwhelm, to dip as by plunging. Literally it means to bury (in water).

By virtue of definition baptism excludes sprinkling or pouring of water over a person, just as one would not sprinkle or pour a little earth over a dead person and say that they were buried.

What is the purpose of water Baptism?

It is for the remission (removal) of sins; **Luke 24:47**, *"And that repentance and remission of sins should be preached in his name among all nations, beginning at Jerusalem."* (Also see **Acts 2:38**).

It is for the washing away of our sins; **Acts 22:16**, *"And now why tarriest thou? arise, and be baptized, and wash away thy sins, calling on the name of the Lord."* (Also see **1 Corinthians 6:11**).

It is a birth of the water (see **John 3:5**) **Titus 3:5**, *"Not by works of righteousness which we have done, but according to his mercy he saved us, by the washing of regeneration, and renewing of the Holy Ghost;"*

It is **a washing** and cleansing of the conscience (1 Peter 3:21), **Hebrews 9:14**, *"How much more shall the blood of Christ, who through the eternal Spirit offered himself*

149

without spot to God, purge your conscience from dead works to serve the living God?"

It is **a burial; Colossians 2:12**, *"Buried with him in baptism, wherein also ye are risen with him through the faith of the operation of God, who hath raised him from the dead."* (**Romans 6:3-4**). A taking on of the Name of Yahoshuah Messiah is coming into Christ (Messiah); **Galatians 3:27**, *"For as many of you as have been baptized into Christ have put on Christ."* (see also **Romans 13:14, James 2:7**).

It is an identification with Him; **Romans 6:3**, *"Know ye not, that so many of us as were baptized into Jesus Christ were baptized into his death?"* (**Galatians 3:27**).

What name should be called over you in baptism?

In **Matthew 28:19** reads, *"Go ye therefore, and teach all nations, baptizing them in the name of the Father, and of the Son, and of the Holy Ghost:"* Yahoshuah said to baptise in the NAME of the Father, the Son and the Holy Ghost.

In **Acts 2:38,** *"Then Peter said unto them, Repent, and be baptized every one of you in the name of Jesus Christ for the remission of sins, and ye shall receive the gift of the Holy Ghost."*

Peter has told us all to baptise in the NAME of Jesus (Yahoshuah) Messiah (Christ). Diligent observation of both verses will reveal that neither: Father, Son, or Holy Ghost are names.

These (so called names) are actually descriptive titles and roles of the one and same Elohim. Therefore when you baptise into the name of Yahoshuah Messiah, you have fulfilled **Matthew 28:19.**

There is no other way to fulfil Yahoshuah's command in **Matthew 28:19**; that is to say, the NAME of the Father and of the Son and of the Holy Ghost means, "in the NAME of Yahoshuah Messiah". Let's look at the pattern and examples of how His apostles carried out this commission to be sure that what we believe totally agrees with scripture.

Yahoshuah tells his disciples to preach repentance and remission of sin in His NAME beginning at Jerusalem (Luke 24:47).

The fulfilment of JESUS' command in **Luke 24:47** and **Matthew 28:19,** is found in **Acts 2:38**. Which is the practical out working of what Yahoshuah had said.

In **Acts 2:38,** they asked the question unto salvation. *"What must I do to be saved?"* The question was a response to the Gospel that Peter preached, and the answer to this genuine response had three parts.

1. **REPENT**

2. **BE BAPTISED IN THE "NAME" OF JESUS CHRIST (YAHOSHUAH MESSIAH)**

3. **RECIEVE THE GIFT OF THE HOLY GHOST.**

Three thousand souls received the Word and were baptised (**Acts 2:41**). How? As Peter had told them what Yahoshuah had commanded.

At Samaria they were baptised in the name of the Lord (Yah) Yahoshuah (Jesus); **Acts 8:12-16**.

Cornelius' household and friends, who had just received the Holy Ghost, were commanded by Peter to be baptised in the name of the Lord (Yahoshuah); who is Lord, Yahoshuah is

Lord; **Acts 10:44-48, Acts 10:36.**

Believers at Ephesus who had been baptised using John the Baptist's formula, were instructed by Paul to be re-baptised in the name of the Lord Yahoshuah (**Acts 19:1-7**).

New Testament believers were always baptised in the name of Jesus Christ (Yahoshuah Messiah). There is not one place or indication that anyone was ever baptised in the New Testament having the titles Father, Son, and Holy Ghost called over them.

The early Church taught that: We should do all things in Yahoshuah's (Jesus') name, (**Colossians 3:17**). They taught that there is salvation in none other than Jesus's (Yahoshuah) name, **Acts 4:12**, and that Yahoshuah has all power in heaven and earth.

Its confirmed in **Matthew 28:18**, *"And Jesus came and spake unto them, saying, All power is given unto me in heaven and in earth."* They taught that there is only one way to be baptised, **Ephesians 4:5**, *"One Lord, one faith, one baptism"*.

How important is water baptism?

Well according to scripture baptism is not just a ritual as some believe, for without baptism in the NAME of Yahoshuah (Jesus) a person retains their sins and thus cannot be saved, why? Because remission of sins is in the name of Yahoshuah (Jesus) and sin cannot enter into the Kingdom of Heaven.

Mark 16:16, *"He that believeth and is baptized shall be saved; but he that believeth not shall be damned."* This scripture points out that it is not he that is saved that then has to be baptised. Rather, he that believes and is therefore baptised shall after the believing act of baptism (in the name) be saved. Does baptism save you? Yes! Baptism does now also save us.

1 Peter 3:21, *"The like figure whereunto even baptism doth also now save us (not the putting away of the filth of the flesh, but the answer of a good conscience toward God,) by the resurrection of Jesus Christ:"* So without the correct baptism, we cannot be saved.

So why do so many baptise their new converts incorrectly?

The number one reason is **false teaching**, **2 Corinthians 11:14-15**, "And no marvel; for Satan himself is transformed into an angel of light. Therefore it is no great thing if his ministers also be transformed as the ministers of righteousness; whose end shall be according to their works." (see **Matthew 7:15-20**). False teaching comes from false teachers.

Wrong traditions, **Colossians 2:8-10**, *"Beware lest any man spoil you through philosophy and vain deceit, after the tradition of men, after the rudiments of the world, and not after Christ. For in him dwelleth all the fulness of the Godhead bodily. And ye are complete in him, which is the head of all principality and power:"* (compare with **Matthew 15:3-9**).

Willful ignorance, **2 Peter 3:5**, *"For this they willingly are ignorant of, that by the word of God the heavens were of old, and the earth standing out of the water and in the water:"* (also **Romans 10:1-3**).

Sincere misunderstanding of scripture. Which is not excused

by Elohim, because to be sincerely wrong is still to be wrong and it is our duty to be diligent and to seek so that we will find. True sincerity will mean that we are seeking but are open to finding the truth at any cost.

Acts 19:2-5 , *"He said unto them, Have ye received the Holy Ghost since ye believed? And they said unto him, We have not so much as heard whether there be any Holy Ghost. And he said unto them, Unto what then were ye baptized? And they said, Unto John's baptism. Then said Paul, John verily baptized with the baptism of repentance, saying unto the people, that they should believe on him which should come after him, that is, on Christ Jesus. When they heard this, they were baptized in the name of the Lord Jesus."* (also **1 Timothy 1:13**).

Part 2 - Birth of the Spirit

Much of Christendom views the Holy Ghost baptism as an optional extra. They think it is a blessing that is not essential to salvation.

However the Bible teaches that receiving the Holy Ghost is absolutely essential to salvation (did you note the word "cannot" in middle of **John 3:5).**

There was also a sound which the Bible indicated would be the same for everyone in **John 3:8**. In **Acts 2:4** we discover that speaking with other tongues is that universal sound, for they all began to speak with other tongues (languages).

What is the Holy Ghost?

It is Elohim Himself coming to dwell in and live through the believer, **1 Corinthians 3:16-17**, *"Know ye not that ye are the temple of God, and that the Spirit of God dwelleth in you? If any man defile the temple of God, him shall God destroy; for the temple of God is holy, which temple ye are."*

In doing this He gives us spiritual life, assures us of our Son ship; and gives us power to witness about Yahoshuah. Not only is Elohim coming to dwell in us, but with His presence also comes His righteousness (right standing). Through the operation of faith, Elohim's very own righteousness becomes ours. The Bible calls this justification.

Who can have the Holy Ghost?

Receiving the Holy Ghost is conditional. When these Bible conditions are met, ANYONE fulfilling the conditions can have this free Gift. Elohim is no respecter of persons, but will give His Holy Ghost to those that ask Him.

Luke 11:13, *"If ye then, being evil, know how to give good gifts unto your children: how much more shall your heavenly Father give the Holy Spirit to them that ask him?"*. Elohim promised the Holy Ghost to all flesh (**Joel 2:28-32**). Peter explained that the Holy Ghost was for the Jews (for you) and for the Gentiles (those that are afar off) and added that it is in fact for anyone that Elohim is calling (**Acts 2:38-39**).

That means that the Holy Ghost is for anyone in Church. It's for anyone in a flesh body, no matter what race or denomination. For this reason Elohim gives the Holy Ghost to them that obey Him, **Acts 5:32**, *"And we are his witnesses of* *these things; and so is also the Holy Ghost, whom God hath given to them that obey him."*

Why some do not receive the Holy Ghost?

There is absolutely no scriptural justification for honest hearted seekers to seek the baptism of the Holy Ghost for weeks, months or even years. Yet some do and for reasons which can be summed up in one word - "ignorance". Let's examine some of the branches of ignorance involved :-

Lack of repentance - God is not free to operate in any set of dishonest circumstances, therefore such a seeker cannot expect to be filled with the Holy Ghost, regardless of how long he/she seeks. A person cannot be honest and cover their sins.

Acts 3:19, *"Repent ye therefore, and be converted, that your sins may be blotted out, when the times of refreshing shall come from the presence of the Lord." (see* **Proverbs 28:13**).

Doubt - When a person prays in doubt, they pray without faith and thus pray to a displeased Elohim; since only faith pleases Elohim.

No meaningful relationship can be established without simple trust between the parties involved. There simply can be no place in heaven for a person that cannot accept that Elohim is wholly truthful.

Elohim is deeply grieved when people doubt him. How? When they doubt His word and refuse to commit themselves to what He has promised or offered (**Hebrews 11:6**).

Preconceived ideas about the experience - The Bible does not say a person will weep, run, laugh, jump or any other reaction when the Holy Ghost is received. One may or may not do any or all of these things, and yet have received the Holy Ghost. The demonstration that accompanies the infilling of the Holy Ghost is determined by the personality of the recipient.

In-spite of everything the Bible offers only one proof of the initial infilling of the Holy Ghost, and that is speaking with other tongues (**Acts 2:4**).

Misguided and misinformed advice and help from well-meaning people -Many well-meaning people of Elohim minister to seekers on the basis of misinformation though truly sincere.

They clearly remember how they were instructed to receive the Holy Ghost, and whether rightly or wrongly they pass it on. This advice is often not scripturally sound and sometimes makes the experience more difficult rather than easier.

The biblical evidence of the Holy Ghost?

On the day of Pentecost which is the birthday of the Church, more than one hundred and twenty people received the Holy Ghost with the supernatural sign of speaking in other tongues as the Spirit gave them utterance.

<u>Acts 2:1-4</u>, *"And when the day of Pentecost was fully come, they were all with one accord in one place. And suddenly there came a sound from heaven as of a rushing mighty wind, and it filled all the house where they were sitting. And there appeared unto them cloven tongues like as of fire, and it sat upon each of them. And they were all filled*

with the Holy Ghost, and began to speak with other tongues, as the Spirit gave them utterance."

Elohim's Word is very precise in giving us, example after example of this phenomenal sign of "speaking with other tongues" (languages) as the evidence one has received the Gift of the Holy Ghost.

Since the turn of the 19th Century it is estimated that at least sixteen million people have received this experience (by now a lot more).

Isaiah prophesied in **Isaiah 28:9-12**, "Whom shall he teach knowledge? and whom shall he make to understand doctrine? them that are weaned from the milk, and drawn from the breasts.

For precept must be upon precept, precept upon precept; line upon line, line upon line; here a little, and there a little: For with stammering lips and another tongue will he speak to this people. To whom he said, This is the rest wherewith ye may cause the weary to rest; and this is the refreshing: yet they would not hear."

The new Testament Church began, with a prayer meeting and the fall of the Holy Ghost upon them followed by being baptised in the Name of Yahoshuah in Water (see **Acts 2:1-29**). This completed the Birth of the Water and the Spirit of which Yahoshuah had spoken in **John 3:5**.

Cornelius' household, who were Gentiles, spoke with other tongues - **Acts 10:44-48**. Believers in John's baptism were re-baptised and spoke with tongues when Paul laid hands on them in **Acts 19:6**.

The importance of the Holy Ghost?

Great stress is made in scripture concerning the importance of the Holy Ghost, if it were not important, would they have been so particular? The reasons are made clear below.

Without the Holy Ghost we will not be caught up, **Romans 8:11**, *"But if the Spirit of him that raised up Jesus from the dead dwell in you, he that raised up Christ from the dead shall also quicken your mortal bodies by his Spirit that dwelleth in you."* (see for more **1Thessalonians 4:16-17**).

Without the Holy Spirit we are none of His **Romans 8:9**, *"But ye are not in the flesh, but in the Spirit, if so be that the Spirit of God dwell in you. Now if any man have not the Spirit of Christ, he is none of his."* (see more **1 Corinthians 12:3; 2 Timothy 2:19**).

Without it we cannot call Yahoshuah Lord (Yah) **1 Corinthians 12:3**, *"Wherefore I give you to understand, that no man speaking by the Spirit of God calleth Jesus accursed: and that no man can say that Jesus is the Lord, but by the Holy Ghost."*

How to receive the gift of the Holy Ghost

1. **Repent** where this has not already been done (Acts 2:38).

2. **Connect** with the Spirit - approach God on the basis of his Love, honour, trustworthiness and other characteristics with the utmost honesty and sincerity Psalm 65:2, *"O thou that hearest prayer, unto thee shall all flesh come"*.

    Again, **Psalm 22:3** says, *"But thou art holy, O thou*

that inhabitest the praises of Israel." And yet again, **Psalm 50:23**, *"Whoso offereth praise glorifieth me: and to him that ordereth his conversation aright will I shew the salvation of God."*

3. **Be Thirsty** (strongly desire it) - **John 7:37-3**9, *"In the last day, that great day of the feast, Jesus stood and cried, saying, If any man thirst, let him come unto me, and drink. He that believeth on me, as the scripture hath said, out of his belly shall flow rivers of living water. (But this spake he of the Spirit, which they that believe on him should receive: for the Holy Ghost was not yet given; because that Jesus was not yet glorified)".*

4. **Come to the Baptiser** (Yahoshuah) - **Matthew 3:11**, *"I indeed baptize you with water unto repentance. but he that cometh after me is mightier than I, whose shoes I am not worthy to bear: he shall baptize you with the Holy Ghost, and with fire:"* (see also **Mark 1:8; Luke 3:16; John 1:33; John 6:37**).

5. **Ask the Father for the Holy Ghost** - **Luke 11:11-13**, *"If a son shall ask bread of any of you that is a father, will he give him a stone? or if he ask a fish, will he for a fish give him a serpent? Or if he shall ask an egg, will he offer him a scorpion? If ye then, being evil, know how to give good gifts unto your children: how much more shall your heavenly Father give the Holy Spirit to them that ask him?"*

6. **Drink** - **John 4:10-15**, *"Jesus answered and said unto her, If thou knewest the gift of God, and who it is that saith to thee, Give me to drink; thou wouldest have asked of him, and he would have given thee living water. The woman saith unto him, Sir, thou hast nothing to draw with, and*

the well is deep: from whence then hast thou that living water? Art thou greater than our father Jacob, which gave us the well, and drank thereof himself, and his children, and his cattle? Jesus answered and said unto her, Whosoever drinketh of this water shall thirst again: But whosoever drinketh of the water that I shall give him shall never thirst; but the water that I shall give him shall be in him a well of water springing up into everlasting life. The woman saith unto him, Sir, give me this water, that I thirst not, neither come hither to draw." (see **Acts 2:1-4**).

7. **Release the outflow: <u>Matthew 12:34-36</u>,** *"O generation of vipers, how can ye, being evil, speak good things? for out of the abundance of the heart the mouth speaketh.*

   A good man out of the good treasure of the heart bringeth forth good things: and an evil man out of the evil treasure bringeth forth evil things. But I say unto you, That every idle word that men shall speak, they shall give account thereof in the day of judgment." (see **Acts 2:4**).

Satan has three objections

1. **You're doing it yourself** (speaking in tongues), ANSWER - **Acts 2:4**, *"And they were all filled with the Holy Ghost, and began to speak with other tongues, as the Spirit gave them utterance."* It's very simple, they were all filled by the Holy Ghost (that's His part of the deal). However, they began to speak in other tongues (that's your part). The Holy Ghost will never force your mouth to speak. You must speak praise in your heart and give utterance to it, but not in English or any language you have ever learned.

If you will praise Elohim in your heart sincerely, and speak what is in your heart to say that is not in any language you have ever learned, you will overcome this objection of the devil and work in a 50/50 partnership where He fills you and you speak it out.

2. **How do you know that you have received the correct spirit?** ANSWER **- Luke 11:13**, *"If ye then, being evil, know how to give good gifts unto your children: how much more shall your heavenly Father give the Holy Spirit to them that ask him?"* You can be sure you will and have received the correct spirt because if you ask Elohim for the right thing, He will not give you a wrong thing and if you ask for a good thing He'll never give a bad thing. In fact, if you ask for the Holy Ghost, you will only get the Holy Ghost.

3. The main thing that candidates aught to beware of that hinders reception of the Holy Spirit however is **SIN**. Sin creates blockages which make it impossible for faith to operate.

   These blockages may be :- Pride, Occult involvement, unforgiveness, wrong relationships, lack of repentance, fear, unbelief, wrong doctrine, analysis paralysis, intellectualism or something else. The answer to sin is simple: Repent!

SUMMARY OF RECIEVING THE HOLY GHOST - **Draw close, ask, drink, release!**

Question? After obeying the Apostles Gospel (Repent, be baptised in Jesus' (Yahoshuah's) name, and receive the gift of the Holy Ghost) am I saved? The answer is an emphatic yes!

Does it end here? No! We must continue in these teachings and build upon them in order to remain saved, **2 Thessalonians 2:15**, *"Therefore, brethren, stand fast, and hold the traditions which ye have been taught, whether by word, or our epistle."* (also read **Acts 2:42**).

The really important question after one is saved according to the Bible should be, "Am I living the baptised life? Have I put away the give and then I'll give you of the "Old Man", and put on the give and take of the "New Man?

1 Corinthians 10:6-10, *"Now these things were our examples, to the intent we should not lust after evil things, as they also lusted. Neither be ye idolaters, as were some of them; as it is written, The people sat down to eat and drink, and rose up to play.*

Neither let us commit fornication, as some of them committed, and fell in one day three and twenty thousand. Neither let us tempt Christ, as some of them also tempted, and were destroyed of serpents. Neither murmur ye, as some of them also murmured, and were destroyed of the destroyer." (see **Colossians 3:1-17**).

The pattern for salvation in the New Testament

120 at Pentecost	Unspoken	Unspoken	Unspoken	Acts 2:4
3000 at Pentecost	Acts 2:41	Acts 2:38	Acts 2:38, 41	Acts 2:38
Samaritans	Acts 8:12	Unspoken	Acts 8:12, 16	Acts 8:27
Eunuch	Acts 8:35	Unspoken	Acts 8:36-38	Unspoken
Saul	Acts 9:5-6	Acts 9:6	Acts 9:18 Acts 22:16 Acts 9:17	1 Cor 14:18
Cornelius	Acts 11:17	Acts 11:18	Acts 10:47-48	Acts 10:44-46
Lydia	Acts 16:14	Unspoken	Acts 16:15	Unspoken
Philippian jailer	Acts 16:30	Acts 16:30	Acts 16:33	Unspoken
Ephesians	Acts 19:1-2	Acts 19:4	Acts 19:5	Acts 19:6

Where ever it is unspoken it is Implied in the text because there are so many witnesses of the fact that the pattern must remain the same. In **Matthew 28:19**, notice again the term, "name," is singular.

The terms, "Father, Son, and Holy Ghost," are not names but titles given to God (Divinity) in His dealings with men. God is our Father because we are His creation; He became the Son of God when He came to earth as our Redeemer robed in flesh; and His Spirit in our life is called the Holy Ghost. According to Scripture, there is only ONE NAME that fulfils this scripture, Yahoshuah also called Jesus.

Ephesians 4:1-6 teaches that there is one Lord, one faith, and one baptism (one way to baptise). The name connected to the Lord is Yahoshuah, the name connected to the faith called Christianity is the name of Messiah (Yahoshuah). The name connected to baptism is again the name, Yahoshuah also called Jesus.

In **Isaiah 42:8; 43:10-11; 44:6, 8; 45:5, 21.** Notice that every description of Elohim is singular. In **Zechariah 14:9** Elohim is One Lord and His name is one! YAHOSHUAH IS THEREFORE THE NAME OF THE:

1. The Father: **Isaiah 9:6; John 5:43; 10:25; Hebrews 1:4,**

2. The Son: **Matthew 1:21; Philippians 2:9-11.**

3. The Holy Ghost: **John 14:18, 26; Romans 8:9; 1 Corinthians 3:17; 13:5; Colossians 1:27; 2:6-7**

Those who are baptised in the name of the Father, Son, and Holy Ghost, are not therefore obeying the command of Jesus, given in **Matthew 28:19**, but rather repeating it again.

For example: If you would go out on a hillside and call out for the rocks to praise God, you would, no doubt, hear an echo of your command, but there would be no obedience. The same is true of those who repeat, or echo, **Matthew 28:19**, rather than obey it. The fulfilment of **Matthew 28:19** is **Acts 2:38.**

Another even clearer example could be, If I am told to go and baptise in the name of the pastor in the Bethnal Green Church, I would certainly ask an important question. What is the name of the pastor of the church in Bethnal Green? Then and only then would I be equipped to carry out the request to baptise others in his name. I would not simply repeat at baptism, "I baptise you in the name of the pastor of the church in Bethnal Green?"

This is what has happened concerning **Matthew 28:19** many are repeating the command parrot fashion without asking the important question of, "What is the name involved in the process." and this needs to be recognised and corrected.

Part 3 - Fire baptism

The third aspect of the work of the Holy Ghost, that is included in the foundation of the Doctrine of Baptisms.

Firstly is the Doctrine of water Baptism which has to do with cleansing. Then there is the Doctrine of the Baptism of the Holy Ghost which is to do with new life and strengthening.

Finally we now consider the Baptism of Fire, which has to do with the quality of life we experience in the Holy Ghost once we begin to serve and follow our Lord Yah.

What is the doctrine of the baptism of fire?

The baptism of fire, also called sanctification or holiness (more specifics in the later lesson on holiness) and this is about separation through such things as trials, tribulations, illness, trouble and persecution, which Elohim uses or allows in our life to bring us to maturity.

The main goal of the baptism of fire is always maturity. The fire baptism begins with the baptism of the Holy Ghost and ends with our lives being separated to God and set apart for His service.

<u>Luke 3:16-17</u>, *"John answered, saying unto them all, I indeed baptize you with water; but one mightier than I cometh, the latchet of whose shoes I am not worthy to unloose: he shall baptize you with the Holy Ghost and with fire: Whose fan is in his hand, and he will throughly purge his floor, and will gather the wheat into his garner; but the chaff he will burn with fire unquenchable."* (**Luke 12:49-52; Acts 14:22**).

Why is it called the baptism of fire?

Fire is a symbol of the Holy Ghost and also a symbol of the purifying judgement of Elohim — **1 Corinthians 3:13,** *"Every man's work shall be made manifest: for the day shall declare it, because it shall be revealed by fire; and the fire shall try every man's work of what sort it is."* (**Acts 2:3**).

Elohim not only wants to burn the chaff out of our lives now — **Luke 3:17,** but He wants to purify (through correction) a people for Himself in whom He can dwell and through whom He can reveal Himself to the world.

Titus 2:14, *"Who gave himself for us, that he might redeem us from all iniquity, and purify unto himself a peculiar people, zealous of good works."* Yahoshuah referred to this separating, purifying, corrective work of the Holy Spirit as the 'Baptism of Fire — **Luke 3:16**.

What is chastening?

Chastening is the corrective work of the Holy Spirit (baptism of fire) through which the Lord (Yah) reveals to us by trials, tribulation and suffering those areas of our character which are weak or in need of change.

Job 23:10, *"But he knoweth the way that I take: when he hath tried me, I shall come forth as gold."* (also see **Isaiah 48:10**). With chastening also comes the grace to change and through heeding this correction we are perfected and drawn closer to Him (**Hebrews 11:4-13**).

Is chastening the same as punishment?

Chastening is not punishment; it is Elohim's love at work in His children. By it He corrects us and leads us into maturity — **John 15:2**, *"Every branch in me that beareth not fruit he taketh away: and every branch that beareth fruit, he purgeth it, that it may bring forth more fruit."* (also **Hebrews 12:5-10**).

Punishment may indeed come, but only if we resist His loving correction now — **Hebrews 10:26-27**, *"For if we sin wilfully after that we have received the knowledge of the truth, there remaineth no more sacrifice for sins, But a certain fearful looking for of judgment and fiery indignation, which shall devour the adversaries."*

What is the result of chastening?

The result of chastening is sanctification, separation or holiness from the World. When Elohim chastens us, we learn the difference between His will or way and our way or will. When we lovingly and trustingly accept His correction, we are then separated (sanctified) from those attitudes and works, which hinder us from becoming and being like Him.

True sanctification is impossible without water baptism, by which we are legally separated from the dominion of sin and self, and through the baptism of the Holy Spirit we are indwell by the Spirit of Elohim, thus becoming "Holy temples of Elohim." — **Matthew 5:48**, *"Be ye therefore perfect, even as your Father which is in heaven is perfect."* (**1 Corinthians 3:16-17; Leviticus 20:26**). So then ultimately chastening works to build holiness into our lives, which is our spiritual strength.

What is the difference between chastening and holiness?

Chastening is what Elohim allows to happen in our life to produce His holiness within us. Holiness is the very nature of Elohim (Elohim is Holy — **Leviticus 19:2**). For every attribute of Elohim stems from who Elohim is: Elohim is love (**1 John 4:8**) and Elohim is Holy.

The essence of holiness is however contained in the principle of love, for true holiness is motivated by love, (**Mark 12:28-31**) e.g. If we love our neighbour as ourselves:

- We will not kill our fellow man.
- We will not steal from them.

- We could not commit adultery with their spouses.

- Nor would we incite lust knowingly in another with whom we come in contact.

This principle requires a change in thinking, behaviour, and even dress code from many of us. Since holiness and love are synonymous (the same) .

2 Chronicles 20:21, *"And when he had consulted with the people, he appointed singers unto the Lord, and that should praise the beauty of holiness, as they went out before the army, and to say, Praise the Lord; for his mercy endureth for ever."* When they praised God's holiness, they actually praised Him for His "Mercy" or love.

Why must we be chastened if Elohim is an Elohim of love?

Without correction and discipline (Baptism of Fire), we will never become partakers of Elohim's holiness, and without holiness we will never see Elohim .

Hebrews 12:14, *"Follow peace with all men, and holiness, without which no man shall see the Lord:"* Sin is that which stops us from being like Elohim. Sin is basically an attack on Elohim's holiness, so it is an attack against Elohim Himself. This means that sin is an offence against Elohim personally.

Psalm 51:4, *"Against thee, thee only, have I sinned, and done this evil in thy sight: that thou mightest be justified when thou speakest, and be clear when thou judgest."* Since belonging to Elohim means being like Him or imitating Him, then those who want to be with Him must also be Holy.

We are not naturally like Elohim, so He could have exercised His option to kill us for offending Him by sinning against Him. However in His Sovereign capacity as Elohim, He decided to change us instead. How? The Baptism of Fire! Through it He cleanses us of everything that displeases Him.

Holiness through fire explained

Holiness is to be separate or different. Holiness is fundamentally the idea of separation, consecration, or devotion to the loving service of Elohim.

It is sharing in Elohim's purity and abstaining from the defilement of the world. For believers it means being separated from the world unto Elohim.

Holiness is both a state of being and a process before Elohim being worked out in the believer's life. As a Christian you are to be holy and through God you're becoming holy. Holiness means loving what Elohim loves and hating what Elohim hates.

It is acting as Messiah would have acted in every situation. The word sanctification is often used in scripture in place of the word holiness (see **1 Peter 1:14-16; Ephesians 5:27; Colossians 1:7**).

Is sanctification progressive or instantaneous?

The process of sanctification begins with righteousness. This right standing is a gift from Elohim to man of the legal right to stand in His presence without guilt, or shame as a result of receiving Yahoshuah as Lord (Yah) and Saviour.

Holiness on the other hand requires effort on the part of the individual believer, while righteousness is a free gift to us. A

171

person may be more holy or less holy, but can only he either right with God (righteous) or in sin (unrighteous).

The remedy for unrighteousness is repentance **1 John 1:9**, *"If we confess our sins, he is faithful and just to forgive us our sins, and to cleanse us from all unrighteousness."* (**Acts 3:19**).

The process of holiness is a joint venture — **Philippians 2:12-13**, *"Wherefore, my beloved, as ye have always obeyed, not as in my presence only, but now much more in my absence, work out your own salvation with fear and trembling. For it is God which worketh in you both to will and to do of his good pleasure."*

Holiness cannot be produced by the efforts of man alone, it takes both the Holy Spirit and the committed believer working together to mature in Holiness. For it involves both the inner and outer man (**1 Corinthians 6:19-20; 1 Thessalonians 5:23**).

Some people today stress outward forms of Holiness like the Pharisees of old (**Matthew 5:20; 2 Corinthians 7:1**).

Others profess inward holiness but Yahoshuah advocates both — **Matthew 23:25-26**, *"Woe unto you, scribes and Pharisees, hypocrites! for ye make clean the outside of the cup and of the platter, but within they are full of extortion and excess.*

Thou blind Pharisee, cleanse first that which is within the cup and platter, that the outside of them may be clean also." The truth is that what is on the inside will always show up on the outside (**Proverbs 23:7**).

Let us finish this lesson off with some principles: -

Treat others the way you would like to be treated, not the way they treat you — **Matthew 7:12**

Whatever thoughts, actions, attitudes, food, clothes etc you wish to have, ask yourself, "Will this bring glory to God? Is this- something I can do, say, etc in the name of Yahosuah? — **1 Corinthians 10:31, Colossians. 3:17.**

Finally ask yourself in every situation, or when faced with a decision, "What would Yahoshuah do? What would Yahoshuah say? What would please Yahoshuah now?

We will return the subject of holiness later as a lesson in its own right in much more depth, so many of the things under the baptism of fire will be repeated again.

Summary

1. We are baptized into Jesus.

2. Jesus baptizes us with the Holy Ghost and with fire.

3. The Holy Ghost baptizes us into one body.

4. Our lives are a life lived in baptism, i.e. laying down our lives to be raised in the power of His resurrection life.

5. These values will help you greatly when applied to your life practically.

6. If you are successful in applying them to your life, you will need less fire to make you like Him but everyone needs fire so there is no escape.

Search the scripture - Fit appropriate scripture to question.

1. What is meant by Baptism?

2. Can someone who is not Born Again enter the Kingdom of Heaven?

3. What name contains Salvation?

4. Which scripture connects - repentance, baptism and the Holy Ghost.

5. Who is identified as the Holy Ghost or Holy Spirit?

6. How many Lord, faiths and baptisms does God's word recognise?

7. What is the initial evidence of baptism in the Holy Ghost?

8. Are we accepted by God as his, without the baptism of the Holy Ghost?

9. In what name are we commanded to do all things?

10. Receiving the Holy Ghost means we receive the power to do what?

2 Corinthians 3:17-18; Romans 8:9; John 3:5; Colossians 3:17; Acts 4:12; Acts 1:8; Ephesians 4:4-6; Acts 2:38; Matthew 3:16; Acts 2:4.

Discussion

1. Have you ever witnessed a baptism, if so, share it with those in your group. If not, what do you imagine it to be like.

2. What is your interpretation of the words, "Holy Ghost"? What is a Ghost and whose Ghost are we speaking of?

3. What is your view about the difference of baptism in the name of Yahoshuah and that of Father, son and Holy Ghost?

4. How have you been baptised and if already baptised how will you go about correcting it?

5. If not baptised at all already either in the name of Yahoshuah or the Holy Ghost, what will you be doing about it?

6. What is the one thing that is the main take away value of this lesson?

Chapter Seven

LAYING ON OF HANDS

Introduction

The Laying on of hands can be defined as an act in which one person places his hand upon the body of another person for some definite spiritual purpose. Normally prayer accompanies this act, by the giving of a prophetic word, or by both.

What is the significance of laying on of hands?

In God's economy, anointed hands become the channel, the vehicle, and the bridge by which something spiritual is transferred, or transmitted, from one person to another. The three key words that are often associated with this concept are:

Identification — through laying on of hands one party identifies, or associates themself with the other. **Leviticus 4:24**, *"And he shall lay his hand upon the head of the goat,* and kill it in the place where they kill the burnt offering before the Lord: it is a sin offering."

Again **Numbers 8:10,** "And thou shalt bring the Levites before the Lord: and the children of Israel shall put their hands upon the Levites:"

Impartation — Through the laying on of hands one party imparts, or transfers, something spiritual to another. **Leviticus 16:21-22,** "And Aaron shall lay both his hands upon the head of the live goat, and confess over him all the iniquities of the children of Israel, and all their transgressions in all their sins, putting them upon the head of the goat,

and shall send him away by the hand of a fit man into the wilderness: And the goat shall bear upon him all their iniquities unto a land not inhabited: and he shall let go the goat in the wilderness."

1 Timothy 4:14, "Neglect not the gift that is in thee, which was given thee by prophecy, with the laying on of the hands of the presbytery." And **Romans 1:11**, "For I long to see you, that I may impart unto you some spiritual gift, to the end ye may be established."

Confirmation — Through the laying on of hands one party confirms, or renders, the other party more firm.

There is a strengthening that takes place — **Leviticus 9:22**, "And Aaron lifted up his hand toward the people, and blessed them, and came down from offering of the sin offering, and the burnt offering, and peace offerings."

And **Acts 14:22**, "Confirming the souls of the disciples and exhorting them to continue in the faith, and that we must

178

through much tribulation enter into the kingdom of God."

What was the Old Testament doctrine of laying on of hands?

The laying on of hands was a means of imparting a blessing — **Genesis 27:26-29**, *"And his father Isaac said unto him, Come near now, and kiss me, my son. And he came near, and kissed him: and he smelled the smell of his raiment, and blessed him, and said, See, the smell of my son is as the smell of a field which the Lord hath blessed:*

Therefore God give thee of the dew of heaven, and the fatness of the earth, and plenty of corn and wine: Let people serve thee, and nations bow down to thee: be lord over thy brethren, and let thy mother's sons bow down to thee: cursed be every one that curseth thee, and blessed be he that blesseth thee."

Genesis 48:13-14,17 , *"And Joseph took them both, Ephraim in his right hand toward Israel's left hand, and Manasseh in his left hand toward Israel's right hand, and brought them near unto him.*

And Israel stretched out his right hand, and laid it upon Ephraim's head, who was the younger, and his left hand upon Manasseh's head, guiding his hands wittingly; for Manasseh was the firstborn."

Verse 17, *"And when Joseph saw that his father laid his right hand upon the head of Ephraim, it displeased him: and he held up his father's hand, to remove it from Ephraim's head unto Manasseh's head."*

Laying on of hands is used for imparting authority. **Numbers 27:15-20, 23**; *"And Moses spake unto the Lord, saying, Let* *the Lord, the God of the spirits of all flesh, set a man over the congregation, Which may go out before them, and which may go in before them, and which may lead them out, and which may bring them in; that the congregation of the Lord be not as sheep which have no shepherd.*

And the Lord said unto Moses, Take thee Joshua the son of Nun, a man in whom is the spirit, and lay thine hand upon him; And set him before Eleazar the priest, and before all the congregation; and give him a charge in their sight.

And thou shalt put some of thine honour upon him, that all the congregation of the children of Israel may be obedient." And **Verse 23**, *"And he laid his hands upon him, and gave him a charge, as the Lord commanded by the hand of Moses."*

Deuteronomy 34:9, *"And Joshua the son of Nun was full of the spirit of wisdom; for Moses had laid his hands upon him: and the children of Israel hearkened unto him, and did as the Lord commanded Moses."*

What is the New Testament doctrine of Laying on of hands?

The New Testament doctrine deals in a fuller sense with the impartation of healing, miracles, the Holy Spirit, the gifts of the Spirit, and the establishment of ministries. Yahoshuah laid the foundation for the New Testament doctrine of healing by:

Laying His hands on those to whom He ministered, **Mark 6:5**, *"And he could there do no mighty work, save that he laid his hands upon a few sick folk, and healed them."* and Luke 4:40, *"Now when the sun was setting, all they that had any* sick with divers diseases brought them unto him; and he laid his hands on every one of them, and healed them." And in **Luke 13:13**, "And he laid his hands on her: and immediately she was made straight, and glorified God."

Passing on spiritual authority to those who have believed upon Him. **Mark 16:15-18**, "And he said unto them, Go ye into all the world, and preach the gospel to every creature. He that believeth and is baptized shall be saved; but he that believeth not shall be damned.

And these signs shall follow them that believe; In my name shall they cast out devils; they shall speak with new tongues; They shall take up serpents; and if they drink any deadly thing, it shall not hurt them; they shall lay hands on the sick, and they shall recover."

The disciples and apostles used this authority given to them by Jesus as they ministered healing and miracles by the laying on of their hands — **Acts 5:12**, "And by the hands of the apostles were many signs and wonders wrought among the people; (and they were all with one accord in Solomon's porch."

And **Acts 9:17**, "And Ananias went his way, and entered into the house; and putting his hands on him said, Brother Saul, the Lord, even Jesus, that appeared unto thee in the way as thou camest, hath sent me, that thou mightest receive thy sight, and be filled with the Holy Ghost."

Laying on of hands is one of the two methods employed by the Lord (Yah) to impart the Baptism of the Holy Spirit **Acts 8:17-19**, "Then laid they their hands on them, and they received the Holy Ghost. And when Simon saw that through laying on of the apostles' hands the Holy Ghost was given, he *offered them money, Saying, Give me also this power, that on whomsoever I lay hands, he may receive the Holy Ghost."*

The laying on of hands is used in the appointment (ordination) of elders and deacons. **Acts 6:6**, *"Whom they set before the apostles: and when they had prayed, they laid their hands on them."*

And **Titus 1:5**, *"For this cause left I thee in Crete, that thou shouldest set in order the things that are wanting, and ordain elders in every city, as I had appointed thee:"*

Laying on of hands is also used in the separating (setting aside or recognising) of believers to a specific work of ministry **Acts 13:2-3**, *"As they ministered to the Lord, and fasted, the Holy Ghost said, Separate me Barnabas and Saul for the work whereunto I have called them. And when they had fasted and prayed, and laid their hands on them, they sent them away."*

The gifts of the Holy Spirit are also imparted by the laying on of hands **2 Timothy 1:16**, *"The Lord give mercy unto the house of Onesiphorus; for he oft refreshed me, and was not ashamed of my chain:"*

What does the Bible admonish us about the laying on of hands?

The Bible warns us to administer the laying on of hands carefully, with discretion and only according to the Word of God and the direction of the Holy Spirit. (**1 Timothy 5:22-24**).

We are to know those who minister to us with the laying on of the hands; i.e., we are to discern that they are "vessels unto honour" and filled with the Holy Ghost (**1 Timothy 5:22**) **1Thessalonians 5:12**, *"And we beseech you, brethren, to know them which labour among you, and are over you in the Lord, and admonish you"*.

Divine healing supplement

Sickness, disease and all forms of suffering came into the world as a result of sin. Because the devil introduced sin into the world, he not Elohim, is the author of all sickness and the suffering that it brings.

Job 2:4-7, *"And Satan answered the Lord, and said, Skin for skin, yea, all that a man hath will he give for his life. But put forth thine hand now, and touch his bone and his flesh, and he will curse thee to thy face. And the Lord said unto Satan, Behold, he is in thine hand; but save his life. So went Satan forth from the presence of the Lord, and smote Job with sore boils from the sole of his foot unto his crown."*

Sin is death at work in our spirits, sickness is death at work in our bodies - **Genesis 2:17**, *"But of the tree of the knowledge of good and evil, thou shalt not eat of it: for in the day that thou eatest thereof thou shalt surely die."*

Has God made a provision for our healing?

Yes! Elohim sent His Son Jesus to redeem every man from the curse of sin of which sickness is a symptom. The blood of Yahoshuah is the satisfaction for our sins and also the means of our healing for every sickness and affliction of body, soul and spirit **Matthew 8:16-17,** *"When the even was come, they brought unto him many that were possessed with devils: and* he cast out the spirits with his word, and healed all that were sick: That it might be fulfilled which was spoken by Esaias the prophet, saying, Himself took our infirmities, and bare our sicknesses."

And **Isaiah 53:5**, "But he was wounded for our transgressions, he was bruised for our iniquities: the chastisement of our peace was upon him; and with his stripes we are healed."

Why is there still so much sickness and disease in the world today?

Because sin is in the world. Only the knowledge and personal acceptance of the fullness of what Christ has done will make the individual free from the power of sin and sicknes.

Hosea 4:6, "My people are destroyed for lack of knowledge: because thou hast rejected knowledge, I will also reject thee, that thou shalt be no priest to me: seeing thou hast forgotten the law of thy God, I will also forget thy children."

James 4:2, "Ye lust, and have not: ye kill, and desire to have, and cannot obtain: ye fight and war, yet ye have not, because ye ask not." And **John 8:32,36**, "And ye shall know the truth, and the truth shall make you free." **Verse 36**, "If the Son therefore shall make you free, ye shall be free indeed."

Can everyone be healed?

Everyone who has heard and believed the Gospel and obeyed it in accordance to (Acts 2:38) can experience the healing power of Yahoshuah Messiah

1 Peter 2:24, *"Who his own self bare our sins in his own body on the tree, that we, being dead to sins, should live unto righteousness: by whose stripes ye were healed."*

Nonbelievers can be healed by faith in Elohim's word, but this is an act of mercy and not a right. Christians have a legal right to be free from sin and sickness. It is therefore Elohim's special gift to believers **Mark 7:27**, *"But Jesus said unto her, Let the children first be filled: for it is not meet to take the children's bread, and to cast it unto the dogs."*

How can we receive healing?

We can receive healing by believing the Word of Elohim and exercising faith in the name of Yahoshuah Messiah **John 16:23-24**, *"And in that day ye shall ask me nothing. Verily, verily, I say unto you, Whatsoever ye shall ask the Father in my name, he will give it you. Hitherto have ye asked nothing in my name: ask, and ye shall receive, that your joy may be full."* And again **Acts 3:6,16**, *"Then Peter said, Silver and gold have I none; but such as I have give I thee: In the name of Jesus Christ of Nazareth rise up and walk."* **Verse 16**, *"And his name through faith in his name hath made this man strong, whom ye see and know: yea, the faith which is by him hath given him this perfect soundness in the presence of you all."*

What means are employed by the Lord to impart healing to us?

The Bible gives us five means by which Elohim delivers us from sickness. They may be used individually or together such as the 'laying on of hands' with the 'gifts of healing'. Because Elohim is sovereign, He is free to move in any way He chooses. Our part is to ask according to His will and then believe **1 John 5:14-15**, *"And this is the confidence that we have in him, that, if we ask any thing according to his will, he heareth us: And if we know that he hear us, whatsoever we ask, we know that we have the petitions that we desired of him."*

The five means of administering healing are as follows:

Personal prayer — **James 5:10,13**, *"Take, my brethren, the prophets, who have spoken in the name of the Lord, for an example of suffering affliction, and of patience."*

<u>**Verse 13**</u>, *"Is any among you afflicted? let him pray. Is any merry? let him sing psalms."* **James 5:16,** *"Confess your faults one to another, and pray one for another, that ye may be healed. The effectual fervent prayer of a righteous man availeth much."*

Prayer and anointing with oil by the elders of the church, <u>**James 5:14-15**</u>, *"Is any sick among you? let him call for the elders of the church; and let them pray over him, anointing him with oil in the name of the Lord: And the prayer of faith shall save the sick, and the Lord shall raise him up; and if he have committed sins, they shall be forgiven him."*

Laying on of hands — **Mark 16:17-18**, *"And these signs shall follow them that believe; In my name shall they cast out devils; they shall speak with new tongues; They shall take up serpents; and if they drink any deadly thing, it shall not hurt them; they shall lay hands on the sick, and they shall recover."*

Gifts of healing — **1 Corinthians 12:1,8-9**, *"Now concerning spiritual gifts, brethren, I would not have you ignorant."* *Verse 8-9, " For to one is given by the Spirit the word of wisdom; to another the word of knowledge by the same*

Spirit; *To another faith by the same Spirit; to another the gifts of healing by the same Spirit;"*

The sent word — **Psalm 107:20**, *"He sent his word, and healed them, and delivered them from their destructions."*

And in **Matthew 8:8**, *"The centurion answered and said, Lord, I am not worthy that thou shouldest come under my roof: but speak the word only, and my servant shall be healed."*

Why do we not always receive healing?

We cannot pretend to have all of the answers, but it would appear from scripture that there are only three reasons:

Ignorance or lack of understanding — **Hosea 4:6**, *"My people are destroyed for lack of knowledge: because thou hast rejected knowledge, I will also reject thee, that thou shalt be no priest to me: seeing thou hast forgotten the law of thy God, I will also forget thy children."*

Unconfessed sin in the life of the individuals seeking healing, especially due to unforgiveness hinders us from receiving healing.

John 5:14, *"Afterward Jesus findeth him in the temple, and said unto him, Behold, thou art made whole: sin no more, lest a worse thing come unto thee."*

And **Matthew 18:34-35**, *"And his lord was wroth, and delivered him to the tormentors, till he should pay all that was due unto him. So likewise shall my heavenly Father do also unto you, if ye from your hearts forgive not every one his brother their trespasses."*

Lack of faith — **Mark 6:5-6**, *"And he could there do no mighty work, save that he laid his hands upon a few sick folk, and healed them. And he marvelled because of their unbelief. And he went round about the villages, teaching."*

Is there a difference between healing and a miracle?

Healing is usually about the restoration of something that is already there, instantly or gradually. Miracles are about replacement or additions of the old with the new in a totally supernatural way.

Christians should not be disappointed because they do not receive an immediately apparent result of healing. Instead pray and act in faith whether you feel healed or not. Faith can only operate where positive attitudes prevail.

Summary

Finally, in summary the laying on of hands is to accomplish five main things — Healing, baptism of the Holy Spirit, Ordination, Setting apart for ministry, impart the gifts of the Spirit. Since casting out demons is a work of healing, sometimes hands are laid upon demonised persons and the force of the Holy Ghost drives them out.

Search the scripture

1. **Mark 9:23** If we believe, what can happen for us?

2. **Luke 10:9** What should we say to the sick when we heal them?

3. **James 5:16** What should we do one for another?

4. **2 Kings 20:5** When did Elohim say he would heal the sick person

5. **Mark 10:52** What made this man whole?

6. **Luke 8:50** What did Jesus say to this man?

7. **Psalm 147:3** What did Elohim do for the broken hearted and wounded.

8. **Luke 13:10-17** What days was it when Yahoshuah healed this woman

9. **Proverbs 17:22** What does a merry heart do for a person?

10. **Malachi 4:2** With what does the Sun of righteousness come?

Discussion

1. What do you see as the most prevalent form of laying of hands?

2. What is your interpretation of laying of hands?

3. Compare laying of hands with not laying hands, can you imagine some situations you should not lay hands on another?

4. How can you practice this teaching safely?

5. What is the most important aspect of this lesson to you?

Chapter Eight

DIVINE HEALTH

Memory Verse

<u>Matthew 8:17</u>, *"That it might be fulfilled which was spoken by Esaias the prophet, saying, Himself took our infirmities, and bare our sicknesses."*

<u>1 Peter 2:24</u>, *"Who his own self bare our sins in his own body on the tree, that we, being dead to sins, should live unto righteousness: by whose stripes ye were healed."*

Introduction

This chapter builds on the chapter about the laying on of hands and so you can expect a certain amount of overlap and repetition, for healing often includes the laying on of hands.

However, what Divine Healing and Health is not is it's not pharmaceutical remedies, imagination, will power, magic, demonology, spiritualism, immunity from dying, presumption, insubordination to Elohim's will, mind over matter, denial of the existence of sin, sickness and disease, or of natural healing by the laws which govern Men's bodies.

What Divine Healing and Health is. It is a definite manifestation of the supernatural power of Elohim in a specific instance to deliver us from any attack by sickness or disease and it is the continued wellness of our physical, mental and spiritual being in the face of attacks by sickness or disease. All of which is based upon faith in Elohim and obedience to Elohim through his Word and the laws He placed in nature to ensure our wellness.

Satan's purpose: concerning the Church has always been to test what we know concerning who we are in Messiah Yahoshuah and just how committed we are to what Elohim has promised.

Our responsibility therefore is to have an accurate knowledge of Elohim's Word (revealed will) so that through knowing what Elohim has said we may be victorious rather than presumptuous. We also have a responsibility to steward our bodies properly by eating, sleeping, exercising and getting our necessary check-ups.

Does Elohim bring sickness and disease to the World? No! It is Satan and not Elohim who brings sickness and disease to the World and the purpose of Yahoshuah is to destroy sickness.

1 John 3:8, *"He that committeth sin is of the devil; for the devil sinneth from the beginning. For this purpose the Son of God was manifested, that he might destroy the works of the devil."* (read **Revelations 12:9; Genesis 3:1-13**). Disobedience to Elohim's Word is what has caused man to inherit pain, sickness and death.

Genesis 3:16-19, *"Unto the woman he said, I will greatly multiply thy sorrow and thy conception; in sorrow thou shalt bring forth children; and thy desire shall be to thy husband,*

and he shall rule over thee. And unto Adam he said, Because thou hast hearkened unto the voice of thy wife, and hast eaten of the tree, of which I commanded thee, saying, Thou shalt not eat of it: cursed is the ground for thy sake; in sorrow shalt thou eat of it all the days of thy life;

Thorns also and thistles shall it bring forth to thee; and thou shalt eat the herb of the field; In the sweat of thy face shalt thou eat bread, till thou return unto the ground; for out of it wast thou taken: for dust thou art, and unto dust shalt thou return." Today the cause of sickness is still the same. Disobedience to Elohim's revealed Word.

Elohim's will concerning Healing

It is important to know what the will of Elohim is concerning healing and once it is known we must hold-fast to His revealed will. Elohim states in His word what His "Highest will and best intention" is concerning man's health. In **3 John 2**, *"Beloved, I wish above all things that thou mayest prosper and be in health, even as thy soul prospereth."*

In this scripture, Elohim makes us to know that He wants us to prosper, be in health and be saved. This is the ideal model that Elohim has left on record for Born again believers, even if we never attain to this it is still true. Elohim wants you well!

Sickness and dis-ease is the equivalent of much broken ease and discomfort in which we or our loved ones are robbed of Joy and wholeness. Sickness is not birthed by love but rather healing comes from our Elohim for He alone is Love.

Disease is an enemy of both Elohim and man. Yahoshuah said that disease was from Satan in **Luke 13:1-17**, *"Whom Satan* *hath bound...be loosed..".* She was bound by Satan but Yahoshuah loosed her.

Acts 10:38 tells us that Yahoshuah went about doing good and healing everyone that was oppressed of the Devil. If disease is the will of Elohim, heaven would be filled with disease and sickness. But Yahoshuah expressed the will of the Father when He went about healing the sick and so must we.

The reason why Elohim came as a Man - Is to deal with the cause of the Curse and its effects, **Genesis 3:15**, *"And I will put enmity between thee and the woman, and between thy seed and her seed; it shall bruise thy head, and thou shalt bruise his heel."* There is a war going on, and many don't even know it. A war for your soul and a war over your body.

The main two reasons are to cause you to be separated from Elohim and be under the authority of sickness and disease. Yahoshuah dealt with it all, the curse is reversed and through Him we are now blessed.

Galatians 3:13-14, *"Christ hath redeemed us from the curse of the law, being made a curse for us: for it is written, Cursed is every one that hangeth on a tree: That the blessing of Abraham might come on the Gentiles through Jesus Christ; that we might receive the promise of the Spirit through faith."* **(Psalm 107:20; Matthew 8:7; 1 Peter 2:24).**

What the Bible teaches concerning Healing

Divine healing is scriptural **(Matthew 8:17; 1 Peter 2:24)**. Health was natural before sin entered the world, **Genesis 1:29-31**, *"And God said, Behold, I have given you every herb bearing seed, which is upon the face of all the earth, and every tree, in the which is the fruit of a tree yielding seed;*

to you it shall be for meat. And to every beast of the earth, and to every fowl of the air, and to every thing that creepeth upon the earth, wherein there is life, I have given every green herb for meat: and it was so. And God saw every thing that he had made, and, behold, it was very good. And the evening and the morning were the sixth day." (also see **Genesis 2:17**).

Death entered through sin as a part of the curse, **Romans 5:12**, *"Therefore, as by one man sin entered into the world, and death by sin; and so death passed upon all men, for that all have sinned:* (Also read **verses 13-21**).

Early promises of redemption prophesied healing through Yahoshuah, (read **Genesis 3:15**). **Isaiah 53:5**, *"But he was wounded for our transgressions, he was bruised for our iniquities: the chastisement of our peace was upon him; and with his stripes we are healed."*

Sickness originated with sin and is part of the kingdom of Satan, **Job 2:6-7**, *"And the Lord said unto Satan, Behold, he is in thine hand; but save his life. So went Satan forth from the presence of the Lord, and smote Job with sore boils from the sole of his foot unto his crown."* (also read, **Matthew 4:23,24; 15:23, 17:14-21; Luke13:16; John 10:10; Acts 10:38**).

The first recorded affliction was the consequence of disobedience, when Elohim's conditions were met healing was given in answer to prayer, (read **Genesis 20:1-18**). Elohim has made a covenant with his people to heal them, **Exodus 15:26**, *"And said, If thou wilt diligently hearken to the voice of the Lord thy God, and wilt do that which is right in his sight, and wilt give ear to his commandments, and keep all his statutes, I will put none of these diseases upon thee,* which I have brought upon the Egyptians: for I am the Lord that healeth thee." (Read **Matthew 23:23; Leviticus 26; Deuteronomy 7:15; 28:1-65; James 5:14-16; Matthew 8:16,17; 1 Peter 2:24**).

Elohim has kept his part of the covenant, **Psalm 103:1-4**, "Bless the Lord, O my soul: and all that is within me, bless his holy name. Bless the Lord, O my soul, and forget not all his benefits: Who forgiveth all thine iniquities; who healeth all thy diseases; Who redeemeth thy life from destruction; who crowneth thee with lovingkindness and tender mercies;" (read **Psalm 105:37; 107:20; Matthew 8:17**).

Healing was promised on the condition of obedience to Elohim's Word. (**Leviticus 26; Deuteronomy 28; Exodus 15:26; Psalm 91**) Psalm 107:17-21, "Fools because of their transgression, and because of their iniquities, are afflicted. Their soul abhorreth all manner of meat; and they draw near unto the gates of death. Then they cry unto the Lord in their trouble, and he saveth them out of their distresses. He sent his word, and healed them, and delivered them from their destructions. Oh that men would praise the Lord for his goodness, and for his wonderful works to the children of men!"

Healing would always come except when there was sin and so people had to live under the curse of the law which had to be upheld (**Leviticus 10; Numbers 25:1-14**); Numbers 11:19-20, "Ye shall not eat one day, nor two days, nor five days, neither ten days, nor twenty days; But even a whole month, until it come out at your nostrils, and it be loathsome unto you: because that ye have despised the Lord which is among you, and have wept before him, saying, Why came we forth out of Egypt?."

The heathen were not promised healing until they fulfilled the terms required for healing such as the Syrophonecian woman (**Matthew 15:21-28**) who lived out faith in the Messiah when it was not available to Gentiles. Only His people have a direct promise from Elohim initially; (**Exodus 15:26**).

Leviticus 26; Deuteronomy 28 prove that all plagues upon Israel occurred because of sin, thus making sin the root cause of sickness.

Think about it, had sin never come into the world, all food, air and water would be health, plus our bodies would not wear out because there everything is everlasting. It is sin that brought about degeneration. Eleven out of the thirteen plagues in the wilderness were caused by misuse of the tongue (read **Exodus 15:24-26; Numbers 32:1-6; Numbers chapters 11-14, 16, 21**).

Elohim did permit Satan to test Job for a time till Job got the revelation of the power of his tongue (read **Job 2:6-7; 3:1,25**). Every time he spoke it was negative that is up until **Job 42:1-7**, *"Then Job answered the Lord, and said, I know that thou canst do every thing, and that no thought can be withholden from thee. Who is he that hideth counsel without knowledge? therefore have I uttered that I understood not; things too wonderful for me, which I knew not. Hear, I beseech thee, and I will speak:*

I will demand of thee, and declare thou unto me. I have heard of thee by the hearing of the ear: but now mine eye seeth thee. Wherefore I abhor myself, and repent in dust and ashes. And it was so, that after the Lord had spoken these words unto Job, the Lord said to Eliphaz the Temanite, My wrath is kindled against thee, and against thy two friends: for ye have not spoken of me the thing that is right, as my servant Job hath." Elohim was dealing with Job about his tongue.

Elohim permitted and still permits Satan to afflict His people when they stray, (Read **Psalm 38; Psalm 103:3; Numbers 12:13-16; 21:1-9**); <u>**Galatians 6:7-8**</u>, "*Be not deceived; God is not mocked: for whatsoever a man soweth, that shall he also reap. For he that soweth to his flesh shall of the flesh reap corruption; but he that soweth to the Spirit shall of the Spirit reap life everlasting.*"

So sickness and affliction are by permission. However the biggest enemy of healing after sin is lack of knowledge <u>**John 8:32**</u>, "*And ye shall know the truth, and the truth shall make you free.*" (read **Hosea 4:6**).

Satan can only successfully put sickness upon a covenant keeping child of Elohim for as long as the Child of Elohim fails to uphold or hold fast to Elohim's Word.

<u>**1 Corinthians 11:29-32**</u>, "*For he that eateth and drinketh unworthily, eateth and drinketh damnation to himself, not discerning the Lord's body. For this cause many are weak and sickly among you, and many sleep. For if we would judge ourselves, we should not be judged.*

But when we are judged, we are chastened of the Lord, that we should not be condemned with the world." (read **1 John 1:7; Psalm 91**).

The excuses of Unbelief

Are people sick for the glory of Elohim? An example quoted is <u>**John 9:1-3**</u>, "*And as Jesus passed by, he saw a man which was blind from his birth. And his disciples asked him, saying,*

198

Master, who did sin, this man, or his parents, that he was born blind? Jesus answered, Neither hath this man sinned, nor his parents: but that the works of God should be made manifest in him." (read **John 11:4**).

Naturally Elohim would not get glory through healing if there were no sickness, yet it is a mistake to think Elohim gets glory from disease apart from healing it, for if sickness were His will He would never oppose it. The Devil would be glorified if sickness could not be healed by Elohim.

Is sickness a chastening from Elohim?

So then anyone who believes sickness glorifies Elohim is presumptuous even to ask Elohim to heal them under the circumstance if sickness be His will. The answer is it is never presumptuous to pray for the covenant blessing promised and granted by Elohim, when we fulfil the conditions. In fact healing is Elohim's name and will (**Exodus 15:26**).

The Greek word for chastening in **Hebrews 12:5-10** is "Paideus" it means child training and has a similar meaning in the other places where it is used. One who confesses to be under the chastening hand of Elohim admits sin and rebellion against Elohim (for this cause an individual falls into the hands of Satan and feels Elohim will do nothing).

However he can still repent and surrender to Elohim who will, forgive him and heal him if he will have faith in Elohim's ability to heal (read **Job 33:14-29; Psalm 38 and Psalm 51).** Where no sin has been committed, and sickness real or imaginary comes against someone, it should be resisted in the name of Yahoshuah and by faith in the finished work of Yahoshuah, (read **James 4:7**) in order to deal with it.

1 Peter 5:8-9, *"Be sober, be vigilant; because your adversary the devil, as a roaring lion, walketh about, seeking whom he may devour: Whom resist stedfast in the faith, knowing that the same afflictions are accomplished in your brethren that are in the world."* Is Elohim the one who sends afflictions? Elohim would not afflict you then ask you to resist; the word affliction is used in many ways in the Bible, even fasting is called afflictions (**Isaiah 58:5**); and only once does affliction clearly refer to sickness (**Psalm 107:17-20**).

Is sickness sent by Elohim?

The fact is Elohim hasn't got any sickness to give anyone. Elohim is life, light and love. Passages such as the following must be understood as being the removal of privileges, when men failed him and sinned.

Nowhere do you read that Elohim did this to those that were true servants and obedient to His will for their life. Such statements are always in connection with rebellion against His Word.

Numbers 14:1-2, *"And all the congregation lifted up their voice, and cried; and the people wept that night. And all the children of Israel murmured against Moses and against Aaron: and the whole congregation said unto them, Would God that we had died in the land of Egypt! or would God we had died in this wilderness!"* Hey guess what, Elohim goes on to oblige them and many of them died. (Read more in **Exodus 15:26; Leviticus 26:14-46;; Deuteronomy 28:20-68; 1 Chronicles 21:14; Job 33:14-29**).

Did healings and miracles all ceased after 64 A.D.? If so then salvation also ceased after the Apostles died. You will find neither of these views in the Bible. Were all the men in the

Bible healed? Not one failure to get healing is recorded where people met the conditions of Elohim.

There never will be a failure where faith is exercised in the Gospel of Elohim. Yahoshuah healed ALL that came to Him and every manner of sickness, (read **Matthew 8:16, 12:15; 14:35-36; Luke 4:10, 10:19; Matthew 4:23-24; 9:35).**

What was Paul's 'thorn' in his flesh? Does it refer to sickness? Some interpret this to mean it is not Elohim's will to heal some people.

In reference to Paul's thorn scripture plainly expounds if we read it in context "An angel of Satan". The Greek word for messenger (in **2 Corinthians 12:7**) means Angel and not disease.

This Angel (demon) followed Paul and caused the troubles listed in **2 Corinthians 11** to keep him humble lest he should be exalted above measure.

The word 'buffet' used in **2 Corinthians 12:7** is never used in connection with sickness else-where in the New Testament (read **Matthew 26:67; 1 Corinthians 4:11; 1 Peter 2:20**).

Therefore whatever was buffeting Paul to keep him humble has to be some supernatural being in order to harmonise scripture. There are other occasions when Elohim has used thorns when referring to some enemy of His People, (**Numbers 33:53; Judges 2:3; Joshua 23:13**).

Four hindrances to faith

Sense of unworthiness - The sense of unworthiness is Satan's attempt to deny the substitutionary sacrifice of Yahoshuah Messiah and your right standing in Messiah, and His righteousness before the Father which was granted to you. Your worthiness depends entirely upon Yahoshuah Messiah the righteous; and you are the righteousness of Elohim in Him (**2 Corinthians 5:21**).

Some settle for hope and mental assent instead of faith. You never hope for the thing you already possess, you hope for the unpossessed. When you hope for healing, it means that you have no faith for it, but you expect to get it sometime in the future.

Mental assent is similar to hope, to mentally declare that the Bible is true from Genesis to Revelation, but never act on it is hypocrisy. Believing means being convicted enough to act on the Word of Elohim, for there is no faith without conviction followed by action.

Sense knowledge evidence is another enemy of healing faith it is when a man believes what he can see. Faith means giving substance to things you have hoped for or expect. Belief is a conviction of the reality of things that are not yet seen, hope relegates what you believe to one day (future) they will happen.

Faith then, changes hope into reality for faith is acting on the Word of Elohim in the face of contrary evidence in the now. Your senses may say "It cannot be", but faith declares "It is and it is now!" Faith counts things as done before Elohim has manifested any physical evidence and this pleases Elohim, for He is a faith responding Elohim.

Unbelief hinders healing because Elohim does not like being called a liar. This is what unbelief is, the act of calling Elohim a liar. Elohim says in His Word we are saved when we have obeyed His Word, the Devil sows doubt in the mind of a person so that they accept what the Devil says above what Elohim has said, thereby making the person to unknowingly take sides with the Devil and become guilty of unbelief.

When Yahoshuah came on the scene as a healer He demanded faith. He declares, *"Thy faith hath made thee whole"*. Again, "All things are possible to him that believeth".

All these statements prove one thing: that all of Yahoshuah's healings were spiritual. He demanded faith, and faith is born of the spirit world, therefore the Word of Elohim is the vehicle of spiritual results.

What about going to the Doctor? The Bible does not teach against Doctors, only against not putting your faith in Elohim to heal you.

King Asa's problem in the passage below was that he looked to the doctor to heal him and not Elohim, **2 Chronicles 16:12**, *"And Asa in the thirty and ninth year of his reign was diseased in his feet, until his disease was exceeding great: yet in his disease he sought not to the Lord, but to the physicians."*

Elohim is not willing for anyone to perish, so He will meet everyone at the level of their faith, but the focus must be on Elohim that heals and not on the tool He uses to accomplish the healing. It must also be understood that while Elohim can and does use doctors to heal, ideally He is most pleased by the direct application of faith in His Word.

Therefore whatever level of faith we are at, our aim must be to attain to total reliance upon Elohim. You can begin right now to apply what you have learnt by starting to exercise your faith at whatever level you are at. Apply your faith to receiving your healing by engaging with Elohim in small ways, e.g. If you have a headache or a pain in some part of your body, why not pray and ask Elohim to heal you rather than take those pills.

Pray against that headache, pain, toothache etc. and build from there. If you feel you require a doctor then pray for Elohim to give you the right doctor and give him/her the wisdom to diagnose correctly and to prescribe the correct medication for your condition and then pray that your recovery will glorify Elohim and confound them as a witness that He did this healing and not them.

Is it right to deny sickness? Nowhere in the Bible does it teach us to deny sickness, Rather it teaches us to affirm our healing. Sickness is a reality, pain and suffering, swelling etc. is a reality.

Yet what Elohim has said is more real than what you can taste, feel, smell, and see; because Elohim's Word is the reason that our physical world exists and it is therefore higher both in nature and authority.

There exists then a conflict in the evidence we perceive. On one hand the evidence of sickness and disease and on the other the evidence of Elohim's Word. Abraham is called the father of faith because he chose to believe Elohim in spite of the evidence presented contrary to Elohim's Word.

He was old, no longer thought about sex never mind having a son at his age. He did not deny the existence of his problems (the sense evidence), he simply refused to stagger by thinking about it and dwelt on what Elohim had said (the promise) instead.

Romans 4:18-25, *"Who against hope believed in hope, that he might become the father of many nations, according to that which was spoken, So shall thy seed be. And being not weak in faith, he considered not his own body now dead, when he was about an hundred years old, neither yet the deadness of Sarah's womb: He staggered not at the promise of God through unbelief; but was strong in faith, giving glory to God;*

And being fully persuaded that, what he had promised, he was able also to perform. And therefore it was imputed to him for righteousness. Now it was not written for his sake alone, that it was imputed to him; But for us also, to whom it shall be imputed, if we believe on him that raised up Jesus our Lord from the dead; Who was delivered for our offences, and was raised again for our justification."

How can I apply what Yahoshuah has done for me on Calvary to receiving my healing or ministering healing to others? I must not stagger at the sense evidence, instead I must hold fast to what the Word of Elohim has said on the subject of healing and expect, be convinced and act like He told me the truth, despite what I see, feel, think or experience. **Hebrews 10:23**, *"Let us hold fast the profession of our faith without wavering; (for he is faithful that promised;)"*

Understand that the reason Elohim heals is not because we are worthy, but because Yahoshuah is worthy and because He loves us and hates Sin, sickness and disease. But while Elohim heals the unsaved because of His great mercy, it is a legal right only for the Child of Elohim (**Matthew 15:26**). If a person expects Elohim to heal him, it is only proper to submit to the Lordship of Yahoshuah and serve Him. One cannot separate the healer from the healing, *"You must be Born* *again"* (**John 3:7**).

In the same way as you had faith in Elohim for forgiveness after that you repented, why not have faith for healing? Refuse to consider even for a moment anything except that Elohim will heal you. Resist all doubt you are healed once you have prayed for (personal prayer) or have been prayed for (someone you trust prayed) concerning your healing.

Just as you resisted when tempted to doubt if Elohim had forgiven you. You accepted Salvation by faith and counted it done whether you felt anything or not. Why? Because you were taught Elohim's promise of Salvation is based upon obedience to His Word, regardless of feelings. Healing too is complete once one has obeyed the Word of Elohim; and likewise we count it as though its done and believe it regardless of feelings, symptoms, or contrary sense evidence.

Stop praying, "If it be thy will?" If you don't know Elohim's will read the Bible. You need to go to Elohim in absolute confidence about those things He has promised. Ask in faith without wavering and results are sure.

James 1:5-8, *"If any of you lack wisdom, let him ask of God, that giveth to all men liberally, and upbraideth not; and it shall be given him. But let him ask in faith, nothing wavering. For he that wavereth is like a wave of the sea driven with the wind and tossed. For let not that man think that he shall receive any thing of the Lord. A double minded man is unstable in all his ways."*

Obey Elohim's Word and serve him in holiness as earnestly as you sought Him; remaining blameless before Elohim is important for our conscience sake so that we don't enter into condemnation of self.

Colossians 2:6-7, *"As ye have therefore received Christ Jesus the Lord, so walk ye in him: Rooted and built up in him, and stablished in the faith, as ye have been taught, abounding therein with thanksgiving."* (see also **John 5:14; 8:11; 1John 3:21-22; 5:14-15; James 4:7; I Peter 5:8-9**).

Keep the peace with your fellow men - "When ye stand praying forgive", **Mark 11:25-26**, *"And when ye stand praying, forgive, if ye have ought against any: that your Father also which is in heaven may forgive you your trespasses. But if ye*

do not forgive, neither will your Father which is in heaven forgive your trespasses." Call for the church Elders to pray for you by all means if you need their support and believe in their prayers but ensure you have forgiven. (see **James 5:14-16; Mark 16:17-20**).

Control your tongue - The mouth of the righteous is a well of life, it has the power to create and to destroy (read **Proverbs 10:19; 12:18; 13:3; 15:4; 16:24; 18:21; Psalm 34:13-14; 1 Pet 3:10-11**).

Live in Elohim and under His protection. **Psalm 91** explains this very well, healing and protection is conditional to dwelling in the secret place of the most High. Therefore control of what we say and declare is important because life and death are in the power of our tongue to produce what we say.

"Death and life are in the power of the tongue: and they that love it shall eat the fruit thereof" **Proverbs 18:21**. In **John 15:7** we read, *"If ye abide in me, and my words abide in you, ye shall ask what ye will, and it shall be done unto you."*

You must use your mouth positively to praise Elohim in faith for healing you before the manifestation can be seen - Forget not all His benefits by bring them to mind through praise. **Psalm 103:1-2**, *"Bless the Lord, O my soul: and all that is within me, bless his holy name. Bless the Lord, O my soul, and forget not all his benefits:"*

Be a faithful steward of your body, don't abuse your body, lose your health then expect God to heal you. That is presumption and not faith, furthermore it's bad stewardship, **1 Corinthians 6:19-20**, *"What? know ye not that your body is the temple of the Holy Ghost which is in you, which ye have of God, and ye are not your own? For ye are bought with a price: therefore glorify God in your body, and in your spirit, which are God's."* (Also read **1 Corinthians 3:16-17**).

Divine physical health

A short word needs to be said about physical health, for being healthy is not all about healing and miracles. However neither do I need to say much about this subject which already has so much written and designed to help people to be naturally healthy (do your own research).

My suggestion here is to find out all you can about living a healthy lifestyle and substitute natural products for synthetic ones whenever you can. Remember that Elohim is not as interested in divine healing as He is in divine health. So look after your temple and stay as healthy as possible naturally.

Firstly, not all illness is about the devil. Many illnesses are the result of personal neglect, overwork, wear and tear and individual abuse. We should not expect to abuse our bodies and have them continue to function correctly nor can we neglect our health and expect to live healthy lives.

Since natural ignorance or laziness got us into a health problem, only by taking responsibility and then taking responsible action can we expect to get back to being healthy again. For in many cases if Elohim healed us supernaturally, we would find ourselves back in the same predicament simply because of repeated poor stewardship.

Secondly our bodies are ours for life. How long our life is, is sometimes dependent on how well we look after our body in terms of hygiene and general care. Bodies require that they are looked after in very much the same way that we manage our time, our money and our skills or abilities.

We want to increase or improve them with use over time, so why don't we have this expectation with our bodies also? It's pretty clear, that if we look after our bodies, the likelihood is our bodies will look after us in return.

Yet we continue to put junk into our bodies for pleasure, abuse them and complain when we get sick or fat? If we want to be healthy, there are some important things we must become conscious of and practice.

The most important components to health is that Yah has built into your body the ability to repair itself as long as it is given the correct building blocks to do the work of restoration and healing.

These are: Adequate sleep, clean water, food, clean air, exercise, adequate clothes for the weather, freedom from too much stress.

Since food, water and air are the main things: we must eat well! Our food should contain: complex carbohydrates, protein, spices for essential minerals, vegetables for minerals and vitamins, water, essential oils preferably from the coconut, chlorophyll, roughage and unsaturated fats. Eat well to live well.

When it comes to water, today we drink a lot of polluted water and can change this simply by purchasing a distiller which is the best form of water purification system available to man today. If you drink bottled water, tap water or even filtered water, you are doing yourself a disservice.

When it comes to air, I do not know about any way we can improve the quality of the air we breathe personally. This is as I understand it a corporate community responsibility.

We have to persuade our communities to plant as many trees as possible and not to cut them down. We need to live as close to forests and greenery as possible. We need to get up early when the air is freshest and exercise.

The body is amazingly tolerant if we give it as many of the building blocks as possible, it will repair itself and keep us healthy for as long as it can even with some shortfalls. When we have exercised good stewardship and the body still breaks down, then we have an absolute right to divine intervention in the form of healings or a miracles.

Summary

1. Divine Healing and Health is the manifestation of the supernatural power of Elohim in a specific instance to deliver us from any attack by sickness or disease.

2. Satan's purpose is to test what we know concerning who we are in Yahoshuah Messiah and just how committed we are to what Elohim has promised.

3. Disobedience to Elohim's Word is what has caused man

to inherit pain, sickness and death.

4. Elohim makes us to know that He wants us to prosper, be in health and be saved.

5. Divine healing is scriptural and spiritual in nature.

6. Remove the hindrances to your faith, like blockages in a stream then your faith can flow freely.

7. Not all illness is due to the devil. Some is the fault of poor stewardship habits.

8. Whereas healing is important, taking care of your health is also.

9. You are entitled to healing or a miracle once you have exercised good stewardship and are in covenant with Elohim.

Search the scripture section - Fit appropriate scripture to questions

1. For what reason did Yahoshuah die? ,

2. What kind of prayer makes a sick person well?

3. How many sick did Yahoshuah heal and with what?

4. What did Yahoshuah say to the person who was unsure of His will to heal?

5. What did Yahoshuah say to the man at the pool?

6. Is every sickness because of sin in someone's life?

7. For what purpose did Yahoshuah come into the world?

8. What is the completion of redemption described as?

9. What is promised if we listen to Elohim and do right in his sight?

10. What is promised if we pay close attention to Elohim's word with sight and heart.

Matthew 8:17; John 9:2,3; Proverbs 4:20-22; 2 Chronicles 16:12; Romans 8:23; John 5:14; Exodus 15:26; 1 John 3:8; Matthew 8:3; James 5:15.

Discussion

1. What are your observations about how we treat our bodies?

2. Define what health means to you?

3. What is the difference between divine health and divine healing?

4. Why is healing from Elohim important at all?

5. What is the devil's role in sickness and disease?

6. How can you apply this lesson to your life today?

Chapter Nine

RESURRECTION OF THE DEAD

Memory Verse

<u>Job 19:25-26</u>, *"For I know that my redeemer liveth, and that he shall stand at the latter day upon the earth: And though after my skin worms destroy this body, yet in my flesh shall I see God:"*

Introduction

The resurrection from the dead is the pivotal point upon which the Gospel of Yahoshuah Messiah rests and without it, His death, burial and resurrection makes no sense and has happened in vain. In short, without the resurrection, we have no Gospel, no Good News and no Christian faith.

However, the Good News is that Yahoshuah did rise from the dead and opened the door for us to eternal life with Him as our Father once again. Of course, this is contingent upon everything else we have studied up until now - repentance, faith, baptism, the laying on of hands and the type of resurrection will be determined in the next study on eternal judgment.

What does it mean to be dead? When the word of Elohim speaks of death, it is speaking of SEPARATION. There are three levels of separation and each is different.

Spiritual separation, <u>Isaiah 59:1-2</u>, *"Behold, the Lord's hand is not shortened, that it cannot save; neither his ear heavy, that it cannot hear: But your iniquities have separated between you and your God, and your sins have hid his face from you, that he will not hear."*

Physical separation, <u>James 2:26</u>, *"For as the body without the spirit is dead, so faith without works is dead also."*

Eternal separation, 2 Thessalonians 1:9, *"Who shall be punished with everlasting destruction from the presence of the Lord, and from the glory of his power;"*

Death in the Bible when spoken of in relation to man, never means ceasing to exist it means separation, and regardless of which category of death you experience, its origin goes back to sin and Satan (read **Romans 5:12-21).**

What does resurrection mean? It means to restore to perfect health and life a body which has no life in itself. Over eight examples are given in the Word of Elohim where dead bodies are resurrected. However this is not what we will be studying for these were all except for one, resurrections unto corruption i.e. temporary resurrections (all these people died again).

Yet the Bible speaks of a "better resurrection" (**Hebrews 11:35**); which is a resurrection unto incorruption it is where death is never faced again. Being raised from death to incorruption means never to die again and is a better resurrection than being resurrected to life and then facing death again.

The resurrection of Yahoshuah Messiah was a resurrection unto incorruption, and it is one of the principles of the Doctrine of Messiah in **Hebrews 6:1-2**. Therefore it is essential to your growth as a Christian to understand this resurrection.

If there be no resurrection of the dead

Two erroneous teachings that Paul had to address because it was overthrowing the faith of some believers was:-

There is no resurrection from the dead - a teaching started through the Sadducees, **Mark 12:18**, *"Then come unto him the Sadducees, which say there is no resurrection; and they asked him, saying,"*

Then there were those who believed that the resurrection was already past, **2 Timothy 2:17-18**, *"And their word will eat as doth a canker: of whom is Hymenaeus and Philetus; Who concerning the truth have erred, saying that the resurrection is past already; and overthrow the faith of some."*

Paul addressed and dismissed both of these false teaching with some facts that questioned whether the line of reasoning used by the false teachers was even logical. He said that if the things preached by the false teachers were true then that meant:-

Messiah is not risen **1 Corinthians 15:13**, *"But if there be no resurrection of the dead, then is Christ not risen"* Is Messiah still dead? No! Our preaching is vain **1 Corinthians 15:14**, *"And if Christ be not risen, then is our preaching vain, and your faith is also vain."* The apostles believe Messiah to have risen or they would not have preached the message so passionately.

Our faith is vain **1 Corinthians 15:17**, *"And if Christ be not raised, your faith is vain; ye are yet in your sins"* They clearly did not believe that they were still in their sins for they preached righteousness and holiness were available to all.

We are false witnesses of God **1 Corinthians 15:15**, *"Yea, and we are found false witnesses of God; because we have testified of God that he raised up Christ: whom he raised not up, if so be that the dead rise not."* They clearly believed their witness was true and their testimony honest. We are yet in our sins (**1 Corinthians 15:17**) The believed their sins were forgiven.

Those asleep (dead), in Messiah have perished **1 Corinthians 15:18**, *"Then they also which are fallen asleep in Christ are perished."* They did not believe this, because they preached the hope of a better resurrection.

We sorrow as others who have no hope (**1 Thessalonians 4:13-18**). They continued to believe in hope against hope or hope even though all the evidence said something different from the Word of Elohim.

In other words because this subject is foundational to our faith as Hebrews. The apostles and disciples continued to believe, because without the resurrection of Yahoshuah Messiah, Christianity would not exist.

The resurrection of the body is a distinctly unique Christian message, and the resurrection of Yahoshuah which is a historic fact which brought life and immortality to life by the Gospel remains central to our faith; **2 Timothy 1:10**, *"But is now made manifest by the appearing of our Saviour Jesus*

Christ, who hath abolished death, and hath brought life and immortality to light through the gospel:"

The Resurrection of Yahoshuah

The fact of Yahoshuah's resurrection is that no one could produce a body but they had a mummy; **John 20:4-10,** *"So they ran both together: and the other disciple did outrun Peter, and came first to the sepulchre.*

And he stooping down, and looking in, saw the linen clothes lying; yet went he not in. Then cometh Simon Peter following him, and went into the sepulchre, and seeth the linen clothes lie, And the napkin, that was about his head, not lying with the linen clothes, but wrapped together in a place by itself.

Then went in also that other disciple, which came first to the sepulchre, and he saw, and believed. For as yet they knew not the scripture, that he must rise again from the dead. Then the disciples went away again unto their own home."

Because of the resurrection of Yahoshuah, we have hope toward Elohim, that there shall be a resurrection of the dead, both of the just and the unjust.

Acts 24:15, *"And have hope toward God, which they themselves also allow, that there shall be a resurrection of the dead, both of the just and unjust."*

Both Yahoshuah and Daniel proclaimed this truth **John 5:29,** *"And shall come forth; they that have done good, unto the resurrection of life; and they that have done evil, unto the resurrection of damnation."*

Daniel 12:2, *"And many of them that sleep in the dust of the earth shall awake, some to everlasting life, and some to shame and everlasting contempt."* There is a great difference between the resurrection of the just and that of the unjust, both in terms of reward and timing;

Revelation 20:5-6, *"But the rest of the dead lived not again until the thousand years were finished. This is the first resurrection. Blessed and holy is he that hath part in the first resurrection: on such the second death hath no power, but they shall be priests of God and of Christ, and shall reign with him a thousand years."* (and **Revelation 20:12-15**).

From this we teach a man born once must die twice, but a man born twice dies only once. Yes! He that is born again and a holy life, against him the second death has no power.

For the resurrection of the just is to decide reward; **1 Corinthians 3:12-15**, *"Now if any man build upon this foundation gold, silver, precious stones, wood, hay, stubble; Every man's work shall be made manifest: for the day shall declare it, because it shall be revealed by fire; and the fire shall try every man's work of what sort it is. If any man's work abide which he hath built thereupon, he shall receive a reward. If any man's work shall be burned, he shall suffer loss: but he himself shall be saved; yet so as by fire."*

But the resurrection of the unjust is a judgement unto death (eternal separation).

Revelation 20:13-15, *"And the sea gave up the dead which were in it; and death and hell delivered up the dead which were in them: and they were judged every man according to their works. And death and hell were cast into the lake of fire. This is the second death. And whosoever was not found*

218

written in the book of life was cast into the lake of fire."

The Word of Elohim clearly teaches the second coming of Yahoshuah Messiah as the coming of Yah. The coming of Yah is most definitely the only hope for any believer. We are waiting for the coming of the Son of Elohim from Heaven but He is really Elohim Himself.

This should be the source of comfort for every believer; **1 Thessalonians 4:17-18**, *"Then we which are alive and remain shall be caught up together with them in the clouds, to meet the Lord in the air: and so shall we ever be with the Lord. Wherefore comfort one another with these words."* (read **John 14:1-3**). It is important to understand that the coming of Yah (the Lord) is in two phases:-

Yahoshuah will be coming back for his people; **Matthew 24:37-44**, *"But as the days of Noah were, so shall also the coming of the Son of man be. For as in the days that were before the flood they were eating and drinking, marrying and giving in marriage, until the day that Noe entered into the ark, And knew not until the flood came, and took them all away; so shall also the coming of the Son of man be.*

Then shall two be in the field; the one shall be taken, and the other left. Two women shall be grinding at the mill; the one shall be taken, and the other left. Watch therefore: for ye know not what hour your Lord doth come. But know this, that if the goodman of the house had known in what watch the thief would come, he would have watched, and would not have suffered his house to be broken up. Therefore be ye also ready: for in such an hour as ye think not the Son of man cometh." (see **1 Thessalonians 4:16-17**).

Yahoshuah will be coming back with his people; **Jude 14**, *"And Enoch also, the seventh from Adam, prophesied of these, saying, Behold, the Lord cometh with ten thousands of his saints,"* (see also 1 Corinthians 6:2-3). Yahoshuah is coming back for His Church.

Paul writing to the Church tells of the Great hope awaiting us in that "Caught up in the air experience" some term the rapture. He makes several things clear to the church concerning this event in **1 Thessalonians 4:13-18** (read).

- Concerning the dead we are not to sorrow as one without hope, v 13.

- Because Yahoshuah rose again he will also raise the dead in Messiah, v14.

- Yah (the Lord) Himself will descend from heaven. There will be a shout from heaven with the voice of the Archangel, and the trumpet of Elohim will sound v16.

- Those who have died living holy lives for Yahoshuah will be raised first, v16.

- Both the living Saints and those who were dead shall be caught up together in the clouds, v17.

- The caught up Saints will meet Yah in the air, never to be parted again, v17.

- We are to comfort one another with this truth, v18.

In **Matthew 24:40-42**, *"Then shall two be in the field; the one shall be taken, and the other left. Two women shall be grinding at the mill; the one shall be taken, and the other* *left. Watch therefore: for ye know not what hour your Lord doth come."*

Yahoshuah spoke of this time and warned of the danger of not being ready. When the Saints are "Caught up" there will be a separation between those who are ready and those who are unprepared.

Two people will be wherever they work or live, one will be taken and the other left, according to **verse 40**. To avoid disappointment we must be alert, **verse 42**.

What Must I Do To Make The First Resurrection?

Paul thought this to be the most important thing he could aim for and said he would do whatever was necessary to make it; **Philippians 3:11**, *"If by any means I might attain unto the resurrection of the dead"*. Bearing this in mind we must understand that qualifying for the resurrection of the DEAD is a three part process. To qualify the process must be completed.

The process is begun the Word of Elohim which is the source of all spiritual life; **Colossians 3:4**, *"When Christ, who is our life, shall appear, then shall ye also appear with him in glory."* (**1 John 3:4; 1 John 5:11-12**).

The start of all spiritual life is when you say yes to the Word, through obedience, (**John 1:1, 14; 1 Peter 1:22-25**). This is the start of what is the rebirth of the Spirit. It occurs when the seed of the Word planted in the heart by the teaching or preaching, of the Word of Elohim is planted (**1 Peter 1:22-25**).

That word became flesh (**John 1:1, 14**); when the hearer obeyed the Gospel according to the Apostles they had received then the Word is manifested (**Acts 2:38**) and thus were saved. This constitutes being born again of the Water and of the Spirit (**John 3:5**).

After being born of the water and of the Spirit, there is no single pursuit that is more important than the renewal of the soul. Every single act of man, however good or bad begins with a thought as taught in (**Proverbs 23:7**). Elohim has declared us "New creatures" in **2 Corinthians 5:17**, but that is not the end.

We are commanded to change our way of thinking **Romans 12:2**, we are to think Elohim's kind of thoughts and live Elohim's kind of life to become transformed. We are to set our affections on things above, that we might be renewed in the knowledge of His image (read **Colossians 3:1-10**), and so thereby qualify for the "rapture".

The battle in our minds decides what happens in the war for our souls. By responding to the Gospel it assures us of our salvation providing we continue to yield to Elohim as He completes the process He started in us in order to bring us to maturity as a Christian. To do this it is important that we:-

Understand that the battle for our mind is spiritual **Ephesians 6:12**, *"For we wrestle not against flesh and blood, but against principalities, against powers, against the rulers of the darkness of this world, against spiritual wickedness in high places."*

The battle ground is in your mind **2 Corinthians 10:3-5**, *"For though we walk in the flesh, we do not war after the flesh: (For the weapons of our warfare are not carnal, but mighty* *through God to the pulling down of strong holds;) Casting down imaginations, and every high thing that exalteth itself against the knowledge of God, and bringing into captivity every thought to the obedience of Christ;"*

The battle ground defined - a conflict between what you know you are in Messiah based on the Word of Elohim, and any thoughts which under cuts, minimises or denies that truth.

Satan seeks to use every available means to win this battle. He stirs up old thought patterns, feelings and reactions from our life before we came to Messiah in an effort to make us prisoners to them again.

The point of conflict - any given situation may be used by the enemy to throw thoughts into our minds, which subtly deny or undercut the truth.

Sometimes the thoughts are a response to a particular situation we find ourselves in but have no control over e.g. Suppose you turn the corner and see a naked person, you have no control over the situation, only what you do next.

At other times they drift into your mind unsolicited and we call these passing thoughts. E.g. You are between sleep and waking, and a thought comes to you, why not kill yourself.

You may never have thought it before, or think it again, but what you choose to do with the thought next defines your future.

You are in control - Satan is the source of the problem thoughts, but it is our responsibility how we handle these thoughts, as and when they arrive in our minds we must judge and dispose of them. Remember it is not a sin to think a sinful thought, it is a sin to entertain a sinful thought.

Ephesians 4:22-24; *"That ye put off concerning the former conversation the old man, which is corrupt according to the deceitful lusts; And be renewed in the spirit of your mind; And that ye put on the new man, which after God is created in righteousness and true holiness."* (read **Colossians 3:2; Philippians 4:8**).

Making war on wrong thoughts

Our criteria for successful warfare against bad thoughts is a knowledge of what God hates and loves (i.e. God's word). The battle we join is against every thought which sets itself against the knowledge of His word and sensitivity to His Spirit.

Using the filter that follows, we can:- **Recognise - Refuse - and Replace**

- Recognise the source of the thought by checking it against what the Word says and what the spirit says to your heart.

- Refuse it entry by resisting it in the name of Yahoshuah, **James 4:7**, *"Submit yourselves therefore to God. Resist the devil, and he will flee from you."*

- Replace the negative, evil, critical or impure thought with Elohim's Word.

Guard the gates of your mind - These are the five gates to your soul; (sight, hearing, taste, touch, smell). As good soldiers guard well, we must guard the gates of our minds.

Guard what you look at; **Matthew 6:22-23**, *"The light of the body is the eye: if therefore thine eye be single, thy whole body shall be full of light. But if thine eye be evil, thy whole body shall be full of darkness. If therefore the light that is in thee be darkness, how great is that darkness!"* (see also **Job 31:1**).

Guard where you go - if you know certain things or places will offer Satan an opportunity to shoot thoughts your way, then don't go there or do it. Guard who you spend your quality time with.

 Proverbs 22:24-25, *"Make no friendship with an angry man; and with a furious man thou shalt not go: Lest thou learn his ways, and get a snare to thy soul."* (**1 Corinthians 15:33**, **Proverbs 27:5-6**).

Guard what you listen to - **Proverbs 20:19**, *"He that goeth about as a talebearer revealeth secrets: therefore meddle not with him that flattereth with his lips."* (**Isaiah 26:3**) this includes music, conversations and passive attention.

Guard your reactions to your feelings **Philippians 4:8**, *"Finally, brethren, whatsoever things are true, whatsoever things are honest, whatsoever things are just, whatsoever things are pure, whatsoever things are lovely, whatsoever things are of good report; if there be any virtue, and if there be any praise, think on these things."* (**Psalm 42:5**).

This type of offensive warfare will immediately reduce the ability of the enemy to sow wrong thoughts into your mind. Be inwardly renewed day by day (**Ephesians 4:23**), and fix your mind on the Word, for only the Word is permanent and everything else is temporary (**2 Corinthians 4:16-18**).

The renewal of the soul is the most important thing after

being born again. It should be the aim of every Christian to be conformed to the image of Messiah. If we fail to do this then we might as well forget about our new bodies.

Resurrection of the body

What will change when Yahoshuah returns, will be our bodies, because with our souls changed, what we need is a new body fit for the changed spirit and soul. So then we will have a new body for our changed character, **Philippians 3:20-21**, *"For our conversation is in heaven; from whence also we look for the Saviour, the Lord Jesus Christ: Who shall change our vile body, that it may be fashioned like unto his glorious body, according to the working whereby he is able even to subdue all things unto himself."*

What will change when Yah comes is the outer shell and not the inner character, we cannot be changed after death, (spirit and soul remain the same) so change now.

Psalm 31:17, *"Let me not be ashamed, O Lord; for I have called upon thee: let the wicked be ashamed, and let them be silent in the grave."* Our bodies will be like His immortal and incorruptible body, (**1 Corinthians 15:15-54**). We will be like the angels.

Luke 20:34-36, *"And Jesus answering said unto them, The children of this world marry, and are given in marriage: But they which shall be accounted worthy to obtain that world, and the resurrection from the dead, neither marry, nor are given in marriage:*

Neither can they die any more: for they are equal unto the angels; and are the children of God, being the children of the resurrection."

Summary

1. The purpose of the resurrection of the dead is a Changed spirit (righteousness) + changed soul (holiness) + changed body = Resurrection of the dead (the result of good stewardship of both spirit and soul is a brand new physical body.

2. We have something to look forward to, something to live for, something to die for and it's worth it because of the resurrection to come. To live is Messiah, but to die is gain as long as we die right with Elohim.

3. We ought not to be afraid of death, only to be prepared to live to die and die right when the time comes, knowing that we will rise again because of what Messiah has done.

Search the Scriptures Section - Fit the appropriate scriptures to questions.

1. What does James say will save our souls?

2. What state of existence describes an unsaved person?

3. When a person is "in Christ" what are they?

4. What qualities will keep you from being ineffective and unproductive?

5. What are we meant to be in this world?

6. Whose minds are blinded to the Gospel?

7. What part of you should be renewed daily?

8. What did Jesus do to Satan's cohorts to show their

total defeat?

9. What shall happen when Jesus returns?

10. What kind of fight are we in?

2 Corinthians 4:3-4; 1 Thessalonians 4:15, 17; Colossians 2:14-15; James 1:22-23; 2 Peter 1:8; 1 Timothy 6:12; Ephesians 2:1-2 Corinthians 4:16; 1 John 4:17; 2 Corinthians 5:17

Discussion

1. What do you think about death?

2. What do you believe happens after death?

3. What is the meaning of resurrection from the dead to you?

4. What is the difference between the resurrection from the dead and any other resurrection?

5. How can we live out this teaching today?

6. What one thing in this lesson has made the biggest difference to you?

Chapter Ten

ETERNAL JUDGEMENT

Introduction

The Word of Elohim tells us that we will one day be held accountable for all that we have done, what we have left undone, and all we have spoken. This is the time when all the joking around stops, all the excuses fade away and we are left with Him to judge us that is the true and living Elohim. There is no escaping it. **Hebrews 9:27** *"... it is appointed unto men once to die, but after this the judgment"*.

We will be looking at this subject area in two parts. Firstly we will look at what is meant by justification and the actual process of justification. Secondly we will examine what Eternal judgement means and how we fit into the scheme of Elohim's plan.

Part 1 - Eternal Judgement

This is essentially the doctrine of Justification (to be just as though you had never sinned). To be made free from the penalty, power and guilt of sin by the application of the blood of Yahoshuah Messiah through His name.

Hebrews 9:22, *"And almost all things are by the law purged with blood; and without shedding of blood is no remission."* And **Luke 24:47**, *"And that repentance and remission of sins should be preached in his name among all nations, beginning at Jerusalem."*

Again **Acts 2:38**, *"Then Peter said unto them, Repent, and be baptized every one of you in the name of Jesus Christ for the remission of sins, and ye shall receive the gift of the Holy Ghost."* This gives one the legal right to stand before Elohim with boldness, without guilt or condemnation as a Son and with the full privileges of Sonship.

John wrote his epistles so that we would know that we have eternal life (the nature of God) and believe upon the name of Yahoshuah, **1 John 5:13**, *"These things have I written unto you that believe on the name of the Son of God; that ye may know that ye have eternal life, and that ye may believe on the name of the Son of God."* Another word for Justified is righteous it could be said that all of this means to be just, fair or right.

Through Yahoshuah, Elohim has rebuked the accusation that He was unfair to create man when He knew he would fall. He has assumed ultimate responsibility by declaring His righteousness through the sacrifice of Messiah that He might be just and the justifier of him that puts faith in Yahoshuah's sacrifice.

Romans 3:26, *"To declare, I say, at this time his righteousness: that he might be just, and the justifier of him which believeth in Jesus."*

For He did not leave man in his condition, but provided a means of Salvation which would meet man's need and by which man could enjoy new life through faith in Yahoshuah Messiah.

Man's need could only be met by receiving Eternal life (the nature of Elohim). However Elohim could not impart to man His very nature and give him the privilege of Sonship, until He can do so on legal grounds. Therefore the first problem He must face is man's need of righteousness (the book of Romans explains this fully).

Elohim's Problem is - He must find a way to declare spiritually dead man (a child of Satan), to be righteous. This involved a threefold problem:-

Elohim must be righteous in all of His dealings with man. Man's transgression must not be overlooked, and the penalty for sin must be paid.

Elohim must act towards Satan on the grounds of absolute justice. He must redeem man from his authority fair and square so that there be no just argument uncovered.

As well as being just to man and Satan Elohim's actions must also satisfy His righteousness without lowering His standards. Legal grounds must be found on which Elohim can justly judge the human race and compel them to pay the penalty of sin if they reject the sacrifice of Yahoshuah on their behalf.

Elohim's Plan in Outline

- Mankind must be redeemed (bought back from Satan) and this redemption must include:-

- Payment in full of Elohim's penalty for Adam's sin.

- Man must be given the spiritual authority by which he can meet Satan and conquer him in just combat.

- A resurrection of man's physical body and immortality must be restored, because man at the beginning had a perfect human body and was not subject to either sickness or death.

- A restoration of the earth to Edenic glory and beauty.

- A recreation of man's spirit to restore him to perfect righteousness and fellowship with Elohim so that he will again feel at home with Elohim.

- Restoration of full privileges and rights as a son, together with the heart acceptance by Elohim of man in His presence and in the midst of His creation.

- We need to know Elohim's judgement spans our past, present and future plus how we can apply this to our Christian life.

Judgement past

I'm a free man as if I had never sinned (fully justified) **Romans 8:1**, *"There is therefore now no condemnation to them which are in Christ Jesus, who walk not after the flesh, but after the Spirit."* Based on my response to what Yahoshuah did on my behalf. The Holy Spirit has convicted me of sin, of righteousness and of judgement, (read **John 16:8-11**).

I responded by obeying the Gospel as preached by the Apostles, (**Acts 2:38**); and I put on Messiah **Galatians 3:27**, *"For as many of you as have been baptized into Christ have put on Christ."* So I now live in a place where Elohim's judgement has already been satisfied and I will be safe providing I remain here (in Messiah, **John 15:4-6**)

I have been justified by His blood and appointed to be saved from wrath through Him, **Romans 5:9,** *"Much more then, being now justified by his blood, we shall be saved from wrath through him."*

So now I reckon myself dead to sin and alive unto Messiah. I will live with Him both now and one day **Romans 6:8**, *"Now if we be dead with Christ, we believe that we shall also live with him:"* I am in Messiah and sin in Messiah has already been judged. So there is now no condemnation for such a one.

Judgement present

Many Christians begin their new life with great zeal and on a spiritual high, but come crashing down the moment Elohim allows them to be touched by divine discipline. Elohim hasn't called us to be converts, but disciples (disciplined ones).

So Christians must learn to undergo Elohim's discipline (training programme) and learn to execute Elohim's judgement upon ourselves, our homes, our congregations and the powers of darkness with confidence now, with stability and assurance through faith.

Elohim has pledged to get you looking just like Yahoshuah **2 Corinthians 3:18**, *"But we all, with open face beholding as in a glass the glory of the Lord, are changed into the same image from glory to glory, even as by the Spirit of the Lord."*

And **Romans 8:29-31**, *"For whom he did foreknow, he also did predestinate to be conformed to the image of his Son, that he might be the firstborn among many brethren. Moreover whom he did predestinate, them he also called: and whom he called, them he also justified: and whom he justified, them he also glorified. What shall we then say to these things? If God be for us, who can be against us?"*

Accept Elohim's judgement on your habits **1 Peter 1:6-7,** *"Wherein ye greatly rejoice, though now for a season, if need be, ye are in heaviness through manifold temptations: That the trial of your faith, being much more precious than of gold that perisheth, though it be tried with fire, might be found unto praise and honour and glory at the appearing of Jesus Christ:"*

Remember it is Elohim's hand (or love and power) controlling the rod of correction **1 Corinthians 10:13**, *"There hath no temptation taken you but such as is common to man: but God is faithful, who will not suffer you to be tempted above that ye are able; but will with the temptation also make a way to escape, that ye may be able to bear it."* (**James 1:12, Matthew 10:22, Hebrews 12: 4-13, Proverbs 20:30**).

Even the good branches get pruned (nothing wrong - no sin but they are pruned to encourage growth), **John 15:2,** *"Every branch in me that beareth not fruit he taketh away: and every branch that beareth fruit, he purgeth it, that it may bring forth more fruit."*

234

You are the house of Yah, **1 Corinthians 3:16-17**, *"Know ye not that ye are the temple of God, and that the Spirit of God dwelleth in you? If any man defile the temple of God, him shall God destroy; for the temple of God is holy, which temple ye are,"* and judgement begins with you. Christians must judge themselves first if they want to set their communities right.

We must judge our motives, thoughts and actions, **Hebrews 4:12**, *"For the word of God is quick, and powerful, and sharper than any twoedged sword, piercing even to the dividing asunder of soul and spirit, and of the joints and marrow, and is a discerner of the thoughts and intents of the heart."*

The Bible teaches us clearly that we are not to judge other people's motives (**Matthew 7:1-2**), for only Elohim knows the motives of the heart.

Jeremiah 17:9-10, *"The heart is deceitful above all things, and desperately wicked: who can know it? I the Lord search the heart, I try the reins, even to give every man according to his ways, and according to the fruit of his doings."* Elohim does however expect us to be like good fruit inspectors and judge the fruits of the behaviours of those we engage (**Matthew 7:1-20**).

Judgement present

Also includes the regulation of the body itself (the Church), **Matthew 18:15-19**, *"Moreover if thy brother shall trespass against thee, go and tell him his fault between thee and him alone: if he shall hear thee, thou hast gained thy brother. But if he will not hear thee, then take with thee one or two more, that in the mouth of two or three witnesses every* *word may be established. And if he shall neglect to hear them, tell it unto the church: but if he neglect to hear the church, let him be unto thee as an heathen man and a publican.*

Verily I say unto you, Whatsoever ye shall bind on earth shall be bound in heaven: and whatsoever ye shall loose on earth shall be loosed in heaven. Again I say unto you, That if two of you shall agree on earth as touching any thing that they shall ask, it shall be done for them of my Father which is in heaven."

Paul in 1 Corinthians 5 puts this process into operation for the benefit of the local Church. This is because those outside the Church judge us based upon those that are known to be among us.

We therefore must be examples to our communities and role models. Our whole purpose in this situation must be the reconciliation of the erring one(s). Failing this the protection of the body from infection and destruction becomes the next priority.

Judgement to come

In (**1 Corinthians 3:11-15**) the Judgement seat of Messiah is portrayed as the place for the examination of the works of believers. At this appointment, Elohim is going to test for the best. He will weigh the bulk of works versus the value of works and quality versus quantity.

He is going to scrutinise our past action by our motives. Believers will have to give account for the things we did and did not do. There is one consolation in that if we are present at that judgement we have made it in the sense that we are

236

saved from eternal separation, yet without reward for the life we lived in the flesh and the things we endured, because our motives were wrong it might be a bitter pill.

Knowing the nature of man's sin, we can understand the reason for the Lake of fire. Both men and angels are eternal. When men and angels become criminals they become eternal criminals. Man is a spirit, and there must be an eternal spirit home available for man. This is true both for the righteous and the unrighteous.

When man became a spiritual criminal, it was necessary that after death he be taken to jail (Hell), to await sentencing (the White Throne judgement). After a court hearing judgement is passed and the proper sentence is executed in this case the judgement is ETERNAL SEPARATION from Elohim in the "Lake of Fire" with the Devil and his angels.

Revelations 20:10-15, *"And the devil that deceived them was cast into the lake of fire and brimstone, where the beast and the false prophet are, and shall be tormented day and night for ever and ever. And I saw a great white throne, and him that sat on it, from whose face the earth and the heaven fled away; and there was found no place for them.*

And I saw the dead, small and great, stand before God; and the books were opened: and another book was opened, which is the book of life: and the dead were judged out of those things which were written in the books, according to their works.

And the sea gave up the dead which were in it; and death and hell delivered up the dead which were in them: and they were judged every man according to their works. And death and hell were cast into the lake of fire. This is the second death. And whosoever was not found written in the book of life was cast into the lake of fire."

Because unsaved man becomes an eternal criminal spiritually there must need be a place of eternal restraint for him. A place where the criminals are segregated from the upright. If they were permitted to roam unrestrained they would demoralise and contaminate the new heaven and earth.

We have prisons for criminals who break the laws of man on earth; We give life imprisonment to serious offenders and habitual criminals. Who then can raise a protest against Elohim if He has a prison in which He restrains those who violate the laws of heaven, and who are eternal criminals?

When man sinned be became a partaker of Satan's nature; as a result Elohim's justice requires satisfaction while His mercy (love) wants to make a way out.

The penalty had to be paid in a way that was legitimate and allow the saved to retain their self-respect, knowing that they were justified on legal grounds. Someone must pay man's penalty so that man can be given eternal life and a bill of right standing before Elohim as though he had never sinned.

This redemption would free man from spiritual separation and the penalty of the Lake of fire. If he refuses it, and persists in His union with Satan, then he must pay the cost of sin for himself. The restoration of righteousness must begin with Elohim since there is no one righteous but He. No man born of natural generation could meet the demands of Justice on behalf of the human race since he too would be a slave to Satan. Yet this redeemer must be a man, however not born of natural generation.

He must be conceived in such a manner that He will not be a subject of Satan. He must not possess within His spirit nature, spiritual death. He must be able to stand before Elohim as the first Adam stood, in righteousness, possessing the same dominion and authority. He must walk on the earth, perfectly pleasing Elohim. He must meet Satan in temptation, as the first man and woman met him, but He must not yield to Satan's will.

This man must then act as a man's substitute. He must meet the demands of justice by taking on Himself man's sin, spiritual death and the judgement of Satan. He must go to prison (Hell). He must remain there, under judgement, until every legal requirement of justice has been fully satisfied against the human race.

He must stay there and suffer until Elohim could legally acquit every human being who takes Him as Saviour and submits to His Lordship. Not only must this Redeemer be free from Satanic dominion in His earth walk, but He must be a being greater than Satan. One who after the penalty had been paid, would be able to conquer Satan, taking from him his lordship and legal dominion over man. He must be able to conquer death and bring life and immortality to light.

2 Timothy 1:10, *"But is now made manifest by the appearing of our Saviour Jesus Christ, who hath abolished death, and hath brought life and immortality to light through the gospel:"*

No angel could act as man's redeemer as an angel could not meet the demands of justice. No man could fulfil the requirements of justice for a redeemer, because of man's union with and subjection to Satan.

Since only Elohim was greater than Satan; Elohim and man had to be united in one individual.

The incarnation was the only answer to man's need for righteousness. Elohim must Himself come as a man and live out His life in measure as a man under the rules he made for men. He must suffer as a man for man, for the accusation was that He had created a man in the face of the fact that He knew he would fall. The responsibility to redeem man was therefore His and only His.

The only way for humanity to be given righteousness was through the incarnation of Elohim. Yahoshuah Messiah the Son of Elohim - Elohim incarnate or Elohim in the flesh **2 Corinthians 5:19**, *"To wit, that God was in Christ, reconciling the world unto himself, not imputing their trespasses unto them; and hath committed unto us the word of reconciliation"*.

Elohim must lay aside His glory and majesty which are rightfully His as Elohim, come to earth and take upon Himself the physical body of a human. He must walk as a son, pleasing the Father, and conquer Satan in his earth walk as a man then, as a man suffer and die to pay the penalty for man's High Treason in man's stead.

When He had paid the penalty for man's treason, He shall acquire by righteous by legal purchase, and that righteousness will become man's.

It was through one man that judgement had come; therefore, one man without sin would be able, on legal grounds, to pay the penalty, so that the human race would be declared free from guilt and unrighteousness if they received the Salvation of the Incarnate One, Yahoshuah Messiah the Righteous one.

In other words, man's need of Eternal Life demanded righteousness and man's need of righteousness demanded the Incarnation.

One day soon Justice will make His demand on man to pay the penalty for his crime, every man outside Messiah will be unable to pay even the interest. The charge is high treason, for an unpardonable sin. The penalty is ETERNAL SEPARATION from Elohim in the LAKE OF FIRE forever and ever.

Judgement for those unsaved - is also to come and that is to condemnation, (read **Revelation 20:10-15 and Revelation 21:7-8**). Eternal Judgement means exactly that, Elohim judges everything past, present and for eternity.

Part Two - The Application of Eternal Judgement

All judgements are not however eternal; some are related to specific eras of time and special matters both temporal and spiritual. Man is obliged to scripturally judge various matters in this life. Eternal Judgement, is the final say and conclusion of the whole matter and is solely in the hands of Elohim.

Some things we can only be trusted to that day when Elohim settles the debates of men. The day when Yahoshuah Messiah, the one true Elohim manifested in the flesh, will sit upon the throne of judgement as the judge of all mankind.

His Word the Bible, will be the book by which we will be judged with every individual of every generation and dispensation standing before Him. Yahoshuah taught Eternal judgement so explicitly that there should be no misunderstanding of what He meant. Every individual of every generation and dispensation will ultimately stand before Elohim in a time of judgement. What happens to us at this judgement is decided by what decisions we have made in this life and our motives in making these decisions. The ultimate decision for which men will be judged is what they did when they heard the Gospel as preached by the Apostles.

Eternal judgement is not to determine whether you are saved or lost; Elohim knows this the moment you die. At death the spirit returns to Elohim who gave it for disposition to either hell or paradise, **Ecclesiastes 12:7**, *"Then shall the dust return to the earth as it was: and the spirit shall return unto God who gave it."*

There the soul of man will wait in temporary bliss or punishment until the resurrection day. If you are saved you will come forth from paradise and take part in the first resurrection. If you are lost you will have part in the second resurrection.

You will come forth to be judged according to the deeds you have done and receive a full reward. Judgement day is the revelation and proclaiming of the secrets of the hearts of men as they stand before Elohim, **Romans 2:16**, *"In the day when God shall judge the secrets of men by Jesus Christ according to my gospel."*

And **1 Corinthians 4:5**, *"Therefore judge nothing before the time, until the Lord come, who both will bring to light the hidden things of darkness, and will make manifest the counsels of the hearts: and then shall every man have praise of God."* The two important segments of eternal judgement need to be examined at this point are:-

The Judgement seat of Messiah - Believers alone will appear at this judgement. The object is not to determine whether you are saved or lost but to determine the extent of your eternal reward, for there is no chance of the raptured ones being separated from the Lord, **1 Thessalonians 4:17**, *"Then we which are alive and remain shall be caught up together with them in the clouds, to meet the Lord in the air: and so shall we ever be with the Lord."*

The white throne judgement - Judgement will be made dispensationally on the basis of works and revealed truth, **Romans 2:11-15**, *"For there is no respect of persons with God. For as many as have sinned without law shall also perish without law: and as many as have sinned in the law shall be judged by the law;*

(For not the hearers of the law are just before God, but the doers of the law shall be justified. For when the Gentiles, which have not the law, do by nature the things contained in the law, these, having not the law, are a law unto themselves:

Which shew the work of the law written in their hearts, their conscience also bearing witness, and their thoughts the mean while accusing or else excusing one another;)" Cain lived before the law of Moses as did many other people. Those whose names are not written in the Book of life will be lost eternally.

Summary

A major lesson to learn here is that it is far better to have your Pastor or brethren gently (sometimes even harshly) correct you now, when they believe you are missing "it" and make a decision to change course now, than to wait for the judgement seat and watch the uncorrected actions or lack of action go into the fire for no reward, **2 Corinthians 5:10**, *"For we must all appear before the judgment seat of Christ;*

that every one may receive the things done in his body, according to that he hath done, whether it be good or bad."

Judgement for the unsaved is also yet to come and that is to condemnation, (read **Revelations 20:10-15, Revelations 21:7-8**). Elohim had a plan in the beginning. He has not given up on that plan even though man has made many mistakes.

He has a plan for mankind, He has a plan for the church and He has a plan for you. Because of sin, we have gone our own way, both individually and corporately. Elohim is in the recovery business, because He loves us. His most prized name is that of Father. You most prized name is child of Elohim.

It is therefore a family issue. In the garden, it looked like He lost His family, but He was willing to sacrifice His own Son for us to get us back. All that He asks is for us to follow these foundational things and we will get back to Him and fulfil all that He has for us on this earth.

The way home:

Repentance	Faith	Baptism
Laying on of Hands	Resurrection	Judgment

This is the way Yahoshuah walked, which makes sense as: *"I am the way, the truth, and the life; no man cometh unto the Father, but by me."* **John 14:6**. This is essentially the doctrine of from sin's guilt by the blood of Jesus or being right with God.

We need to understand that Elohim's Judgements spans our entire and understand how to apply this to our life. I am standing where the fire has already been (explanation due). I am in Christ and sin in Christ has already been judged for all eternity.

Search the scripture

1. For what two reasons did John write his epistles? (**1John 5:13**).

2. Judgement past — I am as if I had never sinned (justified). (**Romans 8:1**).

3. The Judgement of God me (**John 16:8-11**).

4. What are the three steps to salvation contained in the Gospel as preached by the Apostles (**Acts 2:38**).

5. Into what are we baptised (**Galatians 3:27**).

6. What was judged in my past (**Romans 5:9**).

7. What am I to consider myself so that I can have life eternal? (**Romans 6:8**).

8. What is Judgement present mean (**1 Corinthians 11:31**)

9. What kind of death is likely to be the reward of Judgement future if you are unsaved (**Revelations 20:11-15**)

10. What will happen if you are saved but judged to have done works for the wrong motives (**1 Corinthians 3:11-15**)

Discussion

1. What are our natural tendencies when it comes to judging?

2. What is meant by eternal judgement in your mind?

3. Compare the eternal judgement of the saved with that of the unsaved and what do you see as the differences?

4. How can we practically apply this lesson to our lives?

5. What is the single biggest take home value of this lesson for you?

Chapter Eleven

SHARING YOUR FAITH (SOUL-WINNING)

Introduction

Every Christian aught to get the purpose of Yahoshuah Messiah stamped and written upon their heart. We must know and reflect the purpose of our Saviour. Yahoshuah true purpose on earth was to evangelise and disciple those He won to Himself (**Luke 19:10; Matthew 9:13; 1 Timothy 1:15**).

The early church grew to the size it was, mainly because they took the words of Jesus literally, when He said in **Matthew 28:19,** *"Go ye therefore and teach all nations, baptizing them in the name of the Father and of the Son and of the Holy Ghost:"* The latter day church has taken this to mean inviting a sinner to church.

Yes we must invite sinners to the house of Elohim, but to fulfil the Great commission in its fullness, we must learn to share the teaching of the Apostles and disciples when it comes to helping others to know Yahoshuah.

What about teaching soulwinning ?

You might say that teaching this is the pastor's job, let us see what the early church did **Acts 8:1-12**, *"And Saul was consenting unto his death. And at that time there was a great persecution against the church which was at Jerusalem; and they were all scattered abroad throughout the regions of Judaea and Samaria, except the apostles.*

And devout men carried Stephen to his burial, and made great lamentation over him. As for Saul, he made havock of the church, entering into every house, and haling men and women committed them to prison. Therefore they that were scattered abroad went every where preaching the word. Then Philip went down to the city of Samaria, and preached Christ unto them.

And the people with one accord gave heed unto those things which Philip spake, hearing and seeing the miracles which he did. For unclean spirits, crying with loud voice, came out of many that were possessed with them: and many taken with palsies, and that were lame, were healed. And there was great joy in that city. But there was a certain man, called Simon, which beforetime in the same city used sorcery, and bewitched the people of Samaria, giving out that himself was some great one:

To whom they all gave heed, from the least to the greatest, saying, This man is the great power of God. And to him they had regard, because that of long time he had bewitched them with sorceries. But when they believed Philip preaching the things concerning the kingdom of God, and the name of Jesus Christ, they were baptized, both men and women." And Mark 16:15 says, "And he said unto them, Go ye into all the world, and preach the gospel to every creature."

From the above who went? Who would spread the Word ? Who went down to Samaria? We can see that they were all just ordinary saints in the church just like you and me, except for Phillip. This is how it is today, most of us are ordinary saints that do the work of Elohim. A few are gifted evangelists, but all must do their part to progress the work of Yah.

A Witness is one who sees something and is thus able to give a testimony. In the legal sense of the word, it is someone who was personally present at an occurrence and so qualified to give evidence concerning that issue.

Historically it is used in the sense of one who was a spectator of an occasion e.g. a concert. Ethically in the faith, it is applied to someone who is willing to die for their belief in Messiah even though it may mean extreme suffering or a violent death because of what they believe due to their experience of following Messiah.

Principle 1 - The Saints have the ministry of Yahoshuah

The sin of modern Christianity is that we get saved and sit down. We all need to become addicted to soul winning. The ministry of Yahoshuah in every saint is to compel us to meet the needs of a lost and hurting world.

1 Corinthians 16:15, *"I beseech you, brethren, (ye know the house of Stephanas, that it is the firstfruits of Achaia, and that they have addicted themselves to the ministry of the saints,)"*.

Luke 10:2, *"Therefore said he unto them, The harvest truly is great, but the labourers are few: pray ye therefore the Lord of the harvest, that he would send forth labourers into his harvest."*

We received our ministry to the world when we received the Holy Ghost our work is toward wherever we live, London, USA and the uttermost parts of the earth.

Acts 1:8, *"But ye shall receive power, after that the Holy Ghost is come upon you: and ye shall be witnesses unto me both in Jerusalem, and in all Judaea, and in Samaria, and unto the uttermost part of the earth."*

Notice the scripture said 'both', meaning both power and witness in every place. This power and witness comes from the Holy Ghost, the divine power of Elohim working in and through us to accomplish His will (**Matthew 10:1,5-8, 19-20 ; John 4:25-26, 28-30**).

Revelation received and acted upon will turn a sinner into a soul winner **John 12:23-27** (woman at well). The flesh loves revelation but always runs from responsibility.

But the Spirit of Yahoshuah knows His purpose and cause for coming made Him strong to face Gethsemane and Calvary for the sake of the resurrection. "There must be a crucifixion before a resurrection."

Principle 2 - Elohim reconciles through man (2 Corinthians 5:19-20).

Yahoshuah called His disciples out of the world and empowered them so that they could continue His ministry where he left off.

Matthew 10:8, *"Heal the sick, cleanse the lepers, raise the dead, cast out devils: freely ye have received, freely give."* He gave His disciples power and sent them to witness (**Luke 10:19; Matthew 28:18-20**). Yahoshuah had all power and gave the disciples power and commanded them to GO.

Principle 3 - Let's get back to Acts. (Acts 8:1,4).

The Word preached here, means to testify. That is to tell of their experience, and knowledge of Messiah by sharing the Good News.

- At the time who was being persecuted?

- Who was scattered abroad?

- Who was not scattered abroad? (vs. 1)

- What did the church do? (vs. 4)

Elohim gave:- Apostles, Pastors etc. to the Church, to teach the church, to do the work of ministry to the saints. This work is required to make the body increase. **Ephesians 4:12,16**, *"For the perfecting of the saints, for the work of the ministry, for the edifying of the body of Christ:"*

Verse 16, *"From whom the whole body fitly joined together and compacted by that which every joint supplieth, according to the effectual working in the measure of every part, maketh increase of the body unto the edifying of itself in love."*

Principle 4 - Publicly and from house to house (Acts 20: 20-21)

Perfect vision is labelled 20/20 vision the perfect vision of the Church is also 20/20. We should go to where sinners are; publicly in nursing homes, parks, streets, sea sides and from house to house sharing the Good News, seeking and saving the lost.

Too many Christians think that they must know the Bible as well as their pastor before the can teach a Bible Study or talk to a sinner about Yahoshuah.

<u>Acts 4:19-20</u>, *"But Peter and John answered and said unto them, Whether it be right in the sight of God to hearken unto you more than unto God, judge ye. For we cannot but speak the things which we have seen and heard."*

Back then, Bible Christians simply shared their personal experience of salvation and what they were personally taught at every given opportunity with those who needed to hear it.

You can only tell what you know and are sure of. What you don't know you simply answer, "I don't know, but I'll get the answer and get back to you."

That way, you will grow through having to search out answers to questions you never heard before and you will win souls as you grow in the grace of Yahoshuah Messiah.

Witnessing

For witnessing to be successful its focus must be Messiah Yahoshuah. A witness must point seekers to Messiah for Elohim does not exalt denominations, traditions, doctrines, ministries or human personalities. He sends His Spirit to draw souls to Yahoshuah Messiah, **John 16:8**, *"And when he is come, he will reprove the world of sin, and of righteousness, and of judgment:"*.

The witness Elohim gives of Yahoshuah relates to His person, His work and His necessity. Regarding the person of Yahoshuah, the Bible teaches Him to be Elohim in Human flesh form.

Colossians 2:9, *"For in him dwelleth all the fulness of the Godhead bodily."* concerning the work of Yahoshuah, the Bible tells us He came to seek and to save that which was lost, **Luke 19:10**, *"For the Son of man is come to seek and to save that which was lost."*

With reference to His necessity the Bible tells us He is the way, the truth and the life, thus no one can come to the Father (be saved) except through Yahoshuah, (**John 14:6**).

Luke emphasised that it was through His name that when we believed Elohim would remit our sins, **Acts 10:43**, *"To him give all the prophets witness, that through his name whosoever believeth in him shall receive remission of sins."*

Yahoshuah clearly spelled out His plan to the eleven. To the Apostles, He said they should make disciples of all nations; and when they (nations) responded, baptise and then teach them to do those things that He commanded. Get everybody involved, in what Yahoshuah was saying.

Nobody is exempt - evangelisation of the world and the witness of the Gospel is everybody's job. The principle still stands. The primary reason we are saved is to go and save others, and the medium through which this is achieved is the Apostles Gospel.

Therefore in order for us to go and save others we must first be saved by what the Apostles preached then go and save others by preaching the same Gospel.

If I don't know what the Apostles preached or if I have never applied it to my life it is because I am lost,

2 Corinthians 4:3-5, *"But if our gospel be hid, it is hid to them that are lost: In whom the god of this world hath blinded the minds of them which believe not, lest the light of the glorious gospel of Christ, who is the image of God, should shine unto them. For we preach not ourselves, but Christ Jesus the Lord; and ourselves your servants for Jesus' sake."*

Reasons why we aught to witness

You are called to be a witness and commanded to GO, (**Matthew 28:19-20, Mark 16:16, Acts 1:8**).

Understand the outcome of not witnessing – (**John 12:47-48; Revelations 20:10-15, Revelations 21:7-8**).

Why go? - Because if those who know Yahoshuah do not go and take the Gospel, no one else will. Elohim is committed to making disciples from disciples. Therefore to take the Gospel, it takes disciples, even if Elohim has to raise up a fresh group to take it, it will be shared.

Qualifications of a Soul-winner

1. A love for souls, (**Romans 5:5, 2 Corinthians 5:14, Romans 1:14-15**).

2. A personal experience of Salvation, (**John 3:5, Acts 2:38, 1 John 5:13**).

3. In filling of the Holy Ghost, (**Acts 1:8**).

4. The realisation that man is lost without Yahoshuah, (**Luke 19:10, 1 Timothy 1:15**).

5. Practical knowledge of the Bible, (**2 Timothy 3:16-17, 2 Timothy 2:15, Romans 10:17**).

6. Wisdom to deliver the word to the soul, (**Proverbs 14:25, 11:30**).

You have to know someone and something - The Someone that all should know is Yahoshuah and the something is the Gospel. They are inseparable because they are one and the same. The Apostles and disciples of Yahoshuah Messiah were absolutely sure of their testimony therefore so also should we be sure of our faith in Yahoshuah.

1 John 1:3, *"That which we have seen and heard declare we unto you, that ye also may have fellowship with us: and truly our fellowship is with the Father, and with his Son Jesus Christ."*

We are to share this experience in a way that will help others find Yahoshuah, so we must know the key concepts relating to the Gospel. So then, what are the basic truths of the Gospel?

1. The problem of sin is a worldwide problem - All have sinned (**Romans 3:23**).

2. The consequence of sin is separation from Elohim, (**Romans 6:23**).

3. The provision for sin is Yahoshuah, (**John 3:16-21, 2 Corinthians 5:17-21**).

4. The solution for sin is to accept the provision of Yahoshuah, (**Romans 10:13, Romans 10:10**).

5. The way to apply the solution is to identify with Yahoshuah (**Acts 2:38, John 3:5, Mark 16:16**).

The first method of sharing the Gospel is being able to give your testimony

Many Christians do not share their faith because they do not know how to begin. Begin by sharing your Testimony with your unsaved friends. In a testimony you simply share how you came to Yahoshuah Messiah.

The word testimony and sharing also means telling it like or as a witness — (**Acts 1:8**). But ye shall receive power, after that the Holy Ghost is come upon you: and ye shall be witnesses unto me both in Jerusalem, and in all Judaea, and in Samaria, and unto the uttermost part of the earth.

When a Christian witnesses he simply tells what Elohim has done for him. Which is telling what he has seen, heard, and experienced.

<u>Acts 4:20</u>, "For we cannot but speak the things which we have seen and heard". <u>Acts 4:14</u>, *"And beholding the man which was healed standing with them, they could say nothing against it"*. When you give your testimony of Yahoshuah Messiah, simply tell what He means to you.

- What was your life like before conversion?

- How did you receive Messiah?

- What does Messiah mean to you now?

After you have shared your Testimony with a friend, ask the following questions:-

- What is your reaction to that?

- Would you like to receive Yahoshuah Messiah as your Saviour?

- May I show you from the Bible how to receive Yahoshuah Messiah as your Lord and Saviour?

- Turn your Bible to Acts 2:38 — explain what repentance, water baptism in the name of Yahoshuah, and receiving the Holy Ghost means.

- Ask them if they understand, and then if they still want to receive Messiah.

- Tell them it means they are going to repent, be baptised, and be filled with the Holy Ghost. Ask them it they still want to receive Messiah.

If the answer is — Yes! Then pray for them, pray with them and then make an appointment for them to be baptised. Think through your own testimony and jot down the important facts as to what your life was like before you met Messiah.

This will help you speak convincingly of the joy and fulfilment Messiah Yahoshuah brings. A testimony is being able to relate clearly to another what Messiah has done specifically in your life that made you respond to His efforts to win you to Himself.

A good testimony of Yahoshuah contains three perspectives: What your life was like before you met Yahoshuah; What you did to be saved: and what your life with Yahoshuah is like now.

You have to tell something: The Gospel

The second quality of a good witness is that he/she is willing to talk. The problem for many Christians today is they are hindered from talking by self.

One of the leading excuses for not delivering the Gospel is Timidity. Timidity is a serious handicap to Christian service, but it's our duty as well as our privilege as workers together with Elohim to overcome it. Being timid means: easily frightened; lacking confidence; shy; hesitant (**2 Timothy 1:7-8, Jeremiah 1:4-10, Exodus 4:10-12**).

It is a definite obstacle to soulwinning. An understanding of the reason for your fearfulness may well help to show you how to pray and what should be overcome.

As you press on, cultivate the ability to forget your defeats but not your lessons. When you have been unable to lead a soul to Messiah don't be discouraged because you have sown a seed that will grow, continue to pray.

The answer to timidity is boldness. Boldness is simply courage in the face of opposition. Pray for boldness, **Acts 4:29**, *"And now, Lord, behold their threatenings: and grant unto thy servants, that with all boldness they may speak thy word,"*

Main reasons for timidity:-

1. Not sure of your salvation (**2 Timothy 1:12, 1 John 5:12-15, Romans 8:16**).

2. Not having the Holy Ghost (**Acts 1:8**).

3. Neglect of prayer life (**Acts 4:31**).

4. Feelings of inadequacy (**1 Corinthians 1:27**).

5. Lack of knowledge of Elohim's Word (**2 Timothy 2:15**).

6. Lack of confidence in Elohim to work through you (**Philippians 4:13**).

7. Fear of ridicule, (**Galatians 2:20; Acts 5:41**).

8. Lack of practice (**2 Timothy 4:2**).

How to witness

The second approach to soulwinning works with those not apparently in a hurry and with something in your hand like a tract or a sticker or at the very least your Bible (these help you to be more easily identified as a Christian). This is one on one witnessing.

The purpose of witnessing is three fold.

1. To so relate your story that you tell people what they must do to be saved.

2. Secondly to obtain a Bible study to further inform and answer questions.

3. Thirdly to take an opportunity to invite the person to your Church for fellowship.

The big question - If you were to die right now or the moment you started reading this tract, do you have the assurance in your heart that you would go to heaven? This question has but three possible answers. Yes, no or I don't care.

Yes! - Wonderful, so what is it about the Word of Elohim that makes you to know that you are saved? What scripture is that please?

No! - I would like to share with you from the scripture which is the Word of Elohim how you can have that assurance. Is that ok?

I don't care! - Could you tell me what is there about this, that you don't care about, **(Isaiah 59:2, Romans 6:23, Revelations 20:10-15)**.

This form of approach using the big question is only a guideline and not a must, the Holy Ghost will often give you a means of approach to some individuals. Most important is avoiding ambiguous questions like, do you go to Church?

Do however learn to ask questions that will lead to a spiritual discussion. There are always opportunities to witness around us. We aught to have witnessing as a lifestyle, and not allow it to become an additional chore.

Everywhere the Apostles went they witnessed and everywhere they witnessed the Word went. The Word will not go anywhere we don't go so we have to be willing to go everywhere and preach everywhere thereby witnessing becomes be a part of our life. You are to be a witness at home, at work, and abroad whether you like it or not, so you might as well enjoy it (**Acts 1:8**).

Sharing your faith in a deeper way

Openers

- What kind of spiritual background do you come from?

- Are you a Christian?

- What does this mean to you?

Two important Questions?

- Are you absolutely sure that if you were to die today you would go to Heaven?

- If Yahoshuah were to ask you why should I let you into my Heaven, what would you say?

- Would you let me share with you what the Bible says a person needs to do to be sure they will go to Heaven?

The Gospel

Sin was our problem but Elohim has set us free from sin and sickness through Yahoshuah Messiah - **Romans 6:23**, *"For the wages of sin is death; but the gift of God is eternal life through Jesus Christ our Lord"*.

We must respond to what Elohim has done - **John 1:12,** "But as many as received him, to them gave he power to become the sons of God, even to them that believe on his name:"

The Biblical response to the Gospel, Explain repentance, water baptism in the name of Yahoshuah and infilling of the Holy Ghost (**Acts 2:38**).

Afterward ask, "Does this make sense? Is there any aspect of what I have just explained that you do not understand? Next ask: Is there any reason that you can think of right now why you should not give your life to Yahoshuah Messiah now? Would you like to give your life to Yahoshuah Messiah?

What this means is that you are ready to repent of your sins, be baptized in the name of Yahoshuah, and be filled with Elohim's Spirit? Do you still want to make Yahoshuah (Jesus) your Lord and Saviour?

Let's pray; afterwards give them directions and arrange the baptism date, time, place and dress code.

Home bible study

The damning indictment – **Jeremiah 8:20** "we are not saved." There is a world out there waiting to be harvested and only an apostolic can do it – **Matthew 9:37-38; John 4:34-38.** But to sleep in harvest time is a shame - **Proverbs 10:5**

What is home bible study? A programme or lifestyle? (principle) for evangelism or an outreach tool.

- Is it biblical? **Acts 2:46, 5:42, 20:20.**

- What does it take to make it work - prayer, fasting and commitment.

- Committed - Caesar burned ships, tight rope - first few steps

- All living things reproduce. Normal reproduction - one at a time, potentially you can have twins etc, - families.

Biblical principles for soul winning

- Law of the harvest - **Galatians 6:7**

- Fishers of men - **Matthew 4:19**

- What should cause you to go? The commission - called & commanded; **Matthew 28:18-20.**

- Understanding the outcome. – If no-one else will go, it will be hell for the lost.

- There are three kinds of love – but only one leads to action. Have you set goals for souls this year?

- At a bare minimum you should aim to teach just two bible study sessions per week. If you did that you could win a least 1 soul every two months. That represents at least 6 people a year minimum.

- Use these apostolic keys whenever possible - **Acts 2:46**

- Go House to house

- Get involved in providing fellowship for others to get saved.

- Pray consistently for the salvation of souls.

- Share the Word of Elohim regularly and consistently.

Your church has the raw materials for growth and reproduction – you just have to use them.

What is a Home Bible Study (HBS)

Literally, it's a study of the Word of Elohim, given in the home of the seeker. Home Bible Studies are a major tool in the hand of Christians for reaching the lost. Anyone that wants to do HBS can because a HBS is the Word of Elohim.

We systematically set out to explain the Gospel. So no one has a reason to doubt, the success of the Word (Isaiah 55:11) Elohim's Word will not return to Him void (Acts 5:42) . As a car mechanic needs tools to do his job so do the saints of the Most High.

A special task

- Elohim, gives special people and normal people for the work of the ministry (**Ephesians 4:12**).
- What qualifications do I need to be a Home Bible Study teacher.
- You must be born-again according to **Acts 2:38**.
- You must, be living a holy life according to the Bible
- You must become a personal evangelist.

Which one of the following methods was used to Introduce Let us take you to the methods of taking the message of the Gospel by looking at the chart that follows on the next page?

1 Home prayer meetings	6 Bus ministry
2 Street service	7 Door to door invitation
3 Tract ministry	8 Radio or TV broadcast
4 Coffee circle	9 Newspaper Ads.
5 Park service	10 A personal one to meeting e.g. a friend, neighbour, or workmate.

Elohim's law of harvest

Psalms 126:6 says, *"He that cometh forth and weepeth bearing precious seed shall doubtless come again rejoicing, bringing his sheaves with him."* this Is Elohim's law of the harvest. It will work if you work it.

Reasons used for not getting involved in soul-winning:-

- You see no need to

- You do not wish to

- You are afraid to

- You do not know how to.

No doubt you can think of some excuses people use for not getting involved with soulwinning. All the excuses you can think of will fall into one of the above statements. Through Home Bible Studies it is possible to double the size of your church or group in one year.

All you need is for each person to win one soul and because the souls have been won by the Word. They will be more stable. Every church that has methodically employed the ministry of Home Bible Study has grown.

Because you are unfolding the Word of Elohim you stand a better chance of reproducing yourself in others. A Bible study is not hard to teach.

It is just sitting down in a person's home with a Bible and some sheets of paper to unfold what you know about the saving Word of Elohim. Soulwinning is addictive.

Real soul winners continue to win souls no matter where they are and how old they become. They are not super-Christians; they are normal people in Elohim's eyes.

We need to ask ourselves, Why did Elohim save me? "Ye have not chosen me but I have chosen you, and ordained you, that ye should go and bring forth fruit, and that your fruit should remain". (**John 15:16**).

How can we reach the world with the gospel of Yahoshuah Messiah ? Let's start with one soul. At the end of a year there will be two souls.

After two years there will he four souls, after five years there will be 32 souls. After the tenth year there will be 1,048,56 souls won to Elohim the thirty second year would witness 4,294,967,296 people being saved.

Teaching Home Bible Studies

Before you do anything get to prayer and fasting. This will help you to get the priorities of your life right. The best prospects you will recruit for home bible study are the visitors to your church. Other prospects can be found by door knocking, everyday witnessing, street meetings and even advertisements.

The best place to teach the study in in the prospect's home. This is because of the following reasons:

- They are more comfortable in their own home.

- You can leave at will when you are in their home.

- You will not, get as many cancellations to appointments.

It will establish a concept of Elohim in their life after conversion they will not limit Elohim to the church building.

Principles of Home Bible study

1. Always be on time. Use your phone to explain if you are going to be late.

2. If they have a Bible let them use their own, while you read. You must emphasize the authority of the Bible.

3. Dress according to the dress code of your church, casual dress is alright, look your best for Yahoshuah.

4. Be friendly, this will cause people to respond better.

5. It is ok to take a small gift of refreshment.

6. Do not preach your Church, but present Yahoshuah and Him crucified.

7. Always remember your objective is to win to true Bible salvation.

8. Do not allow yourself to be side tracked.

9. Do not teach for too long. This will depend on which study you are teaching.

10. Always complete the study

The do's and don'ts of Home Bible Studies

- Show the fruit, of the Spirit.

- Like begets like so a man should teach a man and a couple should teach a couple.

- The most dedicated saint should be the ones teaching.

- Always open and close in prayer, but not a lengthy prayer either.

- Take time to get familiar with the materials

- Always have a positive attitude.

- don'ts of Home Bible studies

- Don't make the prospect read unless they really want to. You should do this.

- Don't use church language. keep your sharing simple.

- Don't allow yourself to answer judgmentally at any time.

- Don't, run the student's church down.

- Don't make jokes about them, their families or their church. People can be very sensitive and so should you be.

- Don't answer questions that will be answered

- Don't be too authoritative

- Don't carry your troubles of the day into the study

- Don't over-socialise.

Set up a Home Bible Study department for:-

- Visitor follow up use the seven laws of visitor follow up to your advantage.

- Smile - and introduce yourself.

- Be friendly

- The main purpose of the visit or call is to get a home Bible Study!!

- If they are interested in having a Bible Study, report this to your visitor follow up director.

- Invite them back to church

- If they have any special needs report these to the director also.

- Do not talk negatively, complain about anything;

- Remember they are the most important people in Church after Yahoshuah, and should receive our best.

- Don't push your church attendance

New Testament example of Bible studies: **Acts 9:10-18, Acts 13:38-44, Acts 11:1-5.** Paul makes further **Acts 14:21-23.**

Prayer, the vital ingredient

A witness should no more consider going out to witness without praying than a Zoo keeper would consider examining a ferocious Lion in its cage without first sedating it. Prayer gives us power and cover to witness (**Matthew 12:29, Mark 3:27**).

- Pray for the leading and anointing of the Holy Ghost.

- Pray for utterance to speak the Gospel.

- Pray for Elohim to carry out and complete the work that He has begun in their hearts.

Put those you have witnessed to on your prayer list. Put those you know but have not witnessed to on your prayer list (a list of people for whom you desire to pray).

If at all possible pray with and for souls when you have witnessed to them, just make the offer. Afterwards at home continue to pray for all those you have witnessed to that day by name where possible.

Prayer is important for at least four reasons.

1. Prayer prepares the heart to receive Messiah.

2. Prayer opens opportunities to witness, **Colossians 4:2-4.**

3. Specific prayers bring specific answers, **John 13:13-14.**

4. Persistent prayer is rewarded, **Luke 18:1.**

You have to be something

The third quality necessary for a witness is a life that backs up what he says. A holy life is an awesome weapon in the hands of a Holy Elohim.

Romans 16:19, *"For your obedience is come abroad unto all men. I am glad therefore on your behalf: but yet I would have you wise unto that which is good, and simple concerning evil."* The testimony of a known liar or joker in any courtroom is at best laughable and at worse a waste of time.

The most unfortunate thing about non-Christians for Christians is that they don't read the Bible, they read Christians, so that means that as Christians the message we send with our lives must agree with the message the Bible sends about Messiah.

For no one knows better what a Christian should be like than a non-Christian, **2 Corinthians 3:2**, *"Ye are our epistle written in our hearts, known and read of all men:"*

Summary

1. Yahoshuah sent His disciples out 2-by-2 publicly and from house to house.

2. The Apostles continued His ministry and we must continue the ministry of the Apostles by continuing the purpose of Yahoshuah. Evangelise and disciple those you win to the Lord Yah.

3. The process is not finished till those you win are stable and productive in the Kingdom of Elohim. So follow through:

4. Follow up on your witnessing with prayer, telephone calls, letters or visits if appropriate.

5. When you go out specifically for the purpose of witnessing, go two by two where possible, **Luke 10:1**.

6. Encourage those you witness to, to come to Church.

7. Stick to the subject and object of witnessing, Yahoshuah. Steer the conversation gently to Yahoshuah and keep Him in focus.

8. Share your testimony of how Elohim saved you and where He brought you from. Testify in such a way as to point out that if Elohim can do it for you, He can do it for them too. He is no respecter of persons.

Search the Bible section - Fit appropriate scripture to appropriate question.

1. What were the first witnesses told they should preach?

2. What did Yahoshuah command of the man freed from legion?

3. What did the first woman witness say to evangelise a city?

4. If a person has never heard of Yahoshuah, what can't they do?

5. How did Philip start this conversation and how did he steer it to its conclusion?

6. What method of enlightenment did the people of Berea use?

7. In Athens where did Paul go to preach the Gospel?

8. What has Elohim promised His people for their heritage?

9. What did Yahoshuah preach?

10. A person that is wise will do what?

Acts 17:18, 19, Proverbs 11:30, Romans 10:14, Mark 1:15, Acts 17:10, 11, Psalm 11:6, Matthew 10:7, 8, John 4:29, Acts 8:29-38, Luke 8:39.

Discussion

1. How important is soulwinning to you?

2. How do you feel about the unsaved around you and their need to be saved?

3. Compare the different methods of soulwinning and which do you feel most identified with and why?

4. How will you use the info in this chapter to win souls?

5. What sticks in your mind most about this lesson?

Chapter Twelve

STEWARDSHIP (SHARING YOUR RESOURCES)

Memory Verse

<u>Acts 2:42</u>, *"And they continued stedfastly in the apostles' doctrine and fellowship, and in breaking of bread, and in prayers."*

<u>Deuteronomy 8:18</u>, *"But thou shalt remember the Lord thy God: for it is he that giveth thee power to get wealth, that he may establish his covenant which he sware unto thy fathers, as it is this day."*

Introduction

Elohim is no man's debtor. We give to Him with a tea-spoon, He gives to us with a shovel by comparison. Stewardship is about giving. Giving and managing what Elohim has entrusted to us back to Him at the appointed time is stewardship.

He has trusted us with time, treasure, talents and health and it is our responsibility to manage them well for the benefit of Elohim's Kingdom. The side benefit is that we will also prosper and enjoy His blessings as we do.

There Is A Difference Between Ownership and Stewardship. **Psalm 24:1**, *"The earth is the Lord's, and the fulness thereof; the world, and they that dwell therein."* Elohim owns everything, however He has chosen to make us stewards of His creation because of His great love for us. By making us stewards, He demonstrates trust in our ability to learn and to grow.

Stewardship is a divine-human partnership. It is the systematic and proportionate giving of time, abilities and material possessions to Elohim. It is based on conviction that what we receive is on trust from Elohim to be used by in His kingdom and service at the time of His choosing. It's a belief that what we have is not ours, but His.

Stewardship is a way of living that recognises Elohim's Lordship over everything we possess and that our personal resources are to be available for the advancement of Elohim's kingdom's dominion.

Genesis 14:19-22, *"And he blessed him, and said, Blessed be Abram of the most high God, possessor of heaven and earth: And blessed be the most high God, which hath delivered thine enemies into thy hand. And he gave him tithes of all.*

And the king of Sodom said unto Abram, Give me the persons, and take the goods to thyself. And Abram said to the king of Sodom, I have lift up mine hand unto the Lord, the most high God, the possessor of heaven and earth,"

Let us define what a steward is? One who is responsible and accountable for the management of material resources that belong to another, **Matthew 25:24-30**, *"Then he which had received the one talent came and said, Lord, I knew thee* that thou art an hard man, reaping where thou hast not sown, and gathering where thou hast not strawed:

And I was afraid, and went and hid thy talent in the earth: lo, there thou hast that is thine. His lord answered and said unto him, Thou wicked and slothful servant, thou knewest that I reap where I sowed not, and gather where I have not strawed:

Thou oughtest therefore to have put my money to the exchangers, and then at my coming I should have received mine own with usury. Take therefore the talent from him, and give it unto him which hath ten talents. For unto every one that hath shall be given, and he shall have abundance: but from him that hath not shall be taken away even that which he hath. And cast ye the unprofitable servant into outer darkness: there shall be weeping and gnashing of teeth".

The Requirements of Stewardships

Be consistently faithful so that whatever time you are called and checked, that is how you are found to be. **1 Corinthians 4:1-2**, *"Let a man so account of us, as of the ministers of Christ, and stewards of the mysteries of God. Moreover it is required in stewards, that a man be found faithful."*

Psalm 27:14, *"Wait on the Lord: be of good courage, and he shall strengthen thine heart: wait, I say, on the Lord."* Stewards have the patience to wait on their masters for decisions and support without becoming discouraged.

Stewards use their gifts appropriately, **Romans 12:8-12**, *"Or he that exhorteth, on exhortation: he that giveth, let him do it with simplicity; he that ruleth, with diligence; he that* *sheweth mercy, with cheerfulness. Let love be without dissimulation. Abhor that which is evil; cleave to that which is good. Be kindly affectioned one to another with brotherly love; in honour preferring one another; Not slothful in business; fervent in spirit; serving the Lord; Rejoicing in hope; patient in tribulation; continuing instant in prayer"*

Good stewards understand the necessity of and privilege of loving service, **Galatians 5:13**, *"For, brethren, ye have been called unto liberty; only use not liberty for an occasion to the flesh, but by love serve one another."* Love what you do, and love whom you serve, it's the only motive for being a steward of Elohim.

Stewards understand the importance of investing yourself in what you do and how well you serve. The best stewards give of themselves generously knowing that the principle is sure. **Luke 6:38**, *"Give, and it shall be given unto you; good measure, pressed down, and shaken together, and running over, shall men give into your bosom. For with the same measure that ye mete withal it shall be measured to you again."*

Principles for tithes and offerings

Tithes and offerings are not just finance, but include: - Time, talent and treasure and your health and strength.

One principle is to be obedient because you cannot make up by sacrifice what you miss out on by disobedience, **1 Samuel 15:22**, *"And Samuel said, Hath the Lord as great delight in burnt offerings and sacrifices, as in obeying the voice of the Lord? Behold, to obey is better than sacrifice, and to hearken than the fat of rams."* E.g. a big offering instead of giving tithes (won't work). So be obedient and you will be blessed. **Isaiah 1:19** says, *"If ye be willing and obedient, ye shall eat the good of the land:"*

Another principle is to understand giving is like breathing; it's very natural and you can't live without it. It has two parts, breathing in or receiving and breathing out or giving. Put simply it is receive to give and not receive to keep.

Genesis 8:22, *"While the earth remaineth, seedtime and harvest, and cold and heat, and summer and winter, and day and night shall not cease."*

One profound principle is to give Elohim the best of everything they have when it is brought to Him, **Malachi 1:7-8**, *"Ye offer polluted bread upon mine altar; and ye say, Wherein have we polluted thee? In that ye say, The table of the Lord is contemptible.*

And if ye offer the blind for sacrifice, is it not evil? and if ye offer the lame and sick, is it not evil? offer it now unto thy governor; will he be pleased with thee, or accept thy person? saith the Lord of hosts."

It is both a principle and a foundational understanding that You can never out give Elohim. So whatever you give will come back to you sooner or later.

Ecclesiastes 11:1, *"Cast thy bread upon the waters: for thou shalt find it after many days."*

Principles for giving our offerings

Give As Elohim has prospered us **1 Corinthians 16:2**, *"Upon the first day of the week let every one of you lay by him in store, as God hath prospered him, that there be no gatherings when I come."*

Give according to what you have and don't worry about what you don't have. **2 Corinthians 8:12**, *"For if there be first a willing mind, it is accepted according to that a man hath, and not according to that he hath not."*

Give in the same proportion that you would like to receive (generously or sparingly you decide) **2 Corinthians 9:6-7**, *"But this I say, He which soweth sparingly shall reap also sparingly; and he which soweth bountifully shall reap also bountifully. Every man according as he purposeth in his heart, so let him give; not grudgingly, or of necessity: for God loveth a cheerful giver."*

Give as you have made up your mind beforehand to give and not because someone forced or manipulated you to give more or less. Do not give grudgingly because it makes your giving to be in vain and you won't like the results you receive.

Never give out of necessity, that is because you are forced for that also cancels your gift and makes it a resented gift (refer again to **2 Corinthians 9:6-7 above**).

Give cheerfully because you through what Messiah did on the cross are not the same anymore. 2 **Corinthians 8:9**, *"For ye know the grace of our Lord Jesus Christ, that, though he was rich, yet for your sakes he became poor, that ye through his poverty might be rich."* (**2 Corinthians 9:6-7**).

Give with simplicity, don't show off or make a big ceremony when you give, do it quietly and somewhat secretively. Ever seen people who wave their big note around before they give it? **Romans 12:8**, *"Or he that exhorteth, on exhortation: he that giveth, let him do it with simplicity; he that ruleth, with diligence; he that sheweth mercy, with cheerfulness."*

Give because you love Elohim and appreciate what He has done for you. Notice that it was Elohim's love that caused Him to give. **John 3:16**, *"For God so loved the world, that he gave his only begotten Son, that whosoever believeth in him should not perish, but have everlasting life."*

Freewill Offerings

Exodus 35:21, *"And they came, every one whose heart stirred him up, and every one whom his spirit made willing, and they brought the Lord's offering to the work of the tabernacle of the congregation, and for all his service, and for the holy garments."* Freewill giving is the only kind of giving that Elohim values.

Under the Old Covenant, an offering was usually measured at 20% of one's possession. **Leviticus 5:16**, *"And he shall make amends for the harm that he hath done in the holy thing, and shall add the fifth part thereto, and give it unto the priest:*

and the priest shall make an atonement for him with the ram of the trespass offering, and it shall be forgiven him." (**Leviticus 6:5 ; 22:14**). Many times Moses requested an offering. The people gave more than was required and Elohim blessed them for it.

Exodus 36:4-7, *"And all the wise men, that wrought all the work of the sanctuary, came every man from his work which they made; And they spake unto Moses, saying, The people bring much more than enough for the service of the work, which the Lord commanded to make. And Moses gave commandment, and they caused it to be proclaimed throughout the camp, saying, Let neither man nor woman make any more work for the offering of the sanctuary.*

So the people were restrained from bringing. For the stuff they had was sufficient for all the work to make it, and too much." The Bible principle of generous giving always works in the favour of the giver. (read **2 Corinthians 9:6-7** again).

Elohim has set 10% as the necessary payment for tithes (10%) that go to support the ministry. However the offerings ranged from as little as what you have to as much as all that one possessed.

You must decide on what you consider to be a reasonable percentage or amount for an offering from out of your income. However one may give as much as s/he wants out of what the Lord has prospered him with. Offerings are an issue of the heart that demonstrate your love, while tithes demonstrate your obedience. Remember you can't out give Elohim.

More Principles of Giving

1. **Give yourself** to the Lord first **2 Corinthians 8:5**, *"And this they did, not as we hoped, but first gave their own selves to the Lord, and unto us by the will of God."*

2. **Give willingly** 2 Corinthians 8:3,12, **Verse 3,** *"For to their power, I bear record, yea, and beyond their power they were willing of themselves;"* **Verse 12,** *"For if there be first a willing mind, it is accepted according to that a man hath, and not according to that he hath not."*

3. **Give cheerfully** – which means hilariously, **2 Corinthians 9:7b,** *"... for God loveth a cheerful giver."*

4. **Give generously,** liberally (**2 Corinthians 9:7**).

5. **Give proportionately** to how you want to receive, **2 Corinthians 9:6,** *"But this I say, He which soweth sparingly shall reap also sparingly; and he which soweth bountifully shall reap also bountifully."*

6. **Give regularly, 1 Corinthians 16:1-2,** *"Now concerning the collection for the saints, as I have given order to the churches of Galatia, even so do ye. Upon the first day of the week let every one of you lay by him in store, as God hath prospered him, that there be no gatherings when I come"*. The term "First day of the week" implies regularity in giving in worship.

7. **Give systematically** (**2 Corinthians 9:7**) You can systematically increase what you have by investing in a purposeful and systematic way what Elohim has given to you. Regular giving will bring back a blessing regularly.

Then you can increase and give at the new level systematically till you are established and seeing the blessing at your new target level and then you can systematically increase your giving and your receiving this way.

8. **Give thankfully** 2 Corinthians 9:11-12, *"Being enriched in every thing to all bountifulness, which causeth through us thanksgiving to God. For the administration of this service not only supplieth the want of the saints, but is abundant also by many thanksgivings unto God;"*

   Give thankful you don't need that kind of support right now, but knowing that one day you might so be thankful for the opportunity to invest in the future of others for there but for the grace of Elohim do you go.

We should not tithe out of what our Spouse has already tithed on or given to us for the business of the home or even out of money that is not an increase to us such as a loan for business.

What happens if I decide not to give tithes?

Firstly Elohim sees you as a robber (thief) Malachi 3:8-10, *"Will a man rob God? Yet ye have robbed me. But ye say, Wherein have we robbed thee? In tithes and offerings. Ye are cursed with a curse: for ye have robbed me, even this whole nation.*

Bring ye all the tithes into the storehouse, that there may be meat in mine house, and prove me now herewith, saith the Lord of hosts, if I will not open you the windows of heaven, and pour you out a blessing, that there shall not be room enough to receive it."

Secondly you close the windows of heaven upon your own soul thorough disobedience or rebellion to Elohim's Word.

Further, giving tithes is one way of watering seed and storing up treasures in heaven. More to the point it is 'a good measure of what kind of Christian a person is and will become. So we are losers in time and eternity if we fail to tithe — **Proverbs 11:24-25**, *"There is that scattereth, and yet increaseth; and there is that withholdeth more than is meet, but it tendeth to poverty."* (also read **Luke 6:38, Matthew 6:19-21**).

Can I give my tithe as an offering and still have it counted as a tithe?

There is a definite biblical difference between tithes and offerings, (**Malachi 3:8-10**). Elohim's Word teaches us to keep each one in its proper place and not to seek to evade responsibility or create a false impression.

Therefore a tithe given as an offering is not counted in the eyes of man or Elohim as tithe. Neither can one give more than 10% as tithe as only the first 10% counts as a tithe in the eyes of Elohim. The remainder is counted as a voluntary or freewill offering. So a tithe is a tithe and an offering is an offering.

What then is tithing?

The word tithe means a tenth 1/10th. To pay tithes mean giving one tenth e.g. one tenth of the annual increase of lands, material goods etc. or its equivalent in money. We should tithe on all of our income, in the cycle that we get our income (weekly, monthly, quarterly, annually) **Genesis 14:20**, *"And blessed be the most high God, which hath delivered thine enemies into thy hand. And he gave him tithes of all"*.

A biblical practice of returning one tenth of all income back to Elohim, means giving it to your local church; the tithes are required for the upkeep of the ministry (those in ministry). This practice in scripture is not optional but mandatory.

Hebrews 7:5-9, *"And verily they that are of the sons of Levi, who receive the office of the priesthood, have a commandment to take tithes of the people according to the law, that is, of their brethren, though they come out of the loins of Abraham: But he whose descent is not counted from them received tithes of Abraham, and blessed him that had the promises.*

And without all contradiction the less is blessed of the better. And here men that die receive tithes; but there he receiveth them, of whom it is witnessed that he liveth. And as I may so say, Levi also, who receiveth tithes, payed tithes in Abraham." (read **Genesis 14:20** above).

It makes it clear in this scripture above that here on earth **men receive tithes** and that even these men who receive should also pay their tithes. Everyone should tithe, not matter what office they bear or are titled with.

Offerings however are free will gifts given to the local church apart from tithes, it is for the upkeep of the House of the Lord e.g. bills, repairs, purchases, administration etc. (**1 Chronicles 29:9, Psalm 4:5**).

From all of this information we can deduce that tithes are for the living of the ministers, the orphans and widows in the church. While offerings are for the upkeep of the buildings or office etc (bills).

Five points that describe tithing accurately

Mathematically — It is a tenth: <u>**Genesis 28:22**</u>, *"And this stone, which I have set for a pillar, shall be God's house: and of all that thou shalt give me I will surely give the tenth unto thee."* And again, <u>**Leviticus 27:30**</u>, *"And all the tithe of the land, whether of the seed of the land, or of the fruit of the tree, is the Lord's: it is holy unto the Lord."*

Scripturally — It is a law: <u>**Deuteronomy 12:6**</u>, *"And thither ye shall bring your burnt offerings, and your sacrifices, and your tithes, and heave offerings of your hand, and your vows, and your freewill offerings, and the firstlings of your herds and of your flocks:"*

And <u>**Deuteronomy 14:22**</u>, *"Thou shalt truly tithe all the increase of thy seed, that the field bringeth forth year by year."*

Morally — It is a debt: <u>**Malachi 3:8**</u>, *"Will a man rob God? Yet ye have robbed me. But ye say, Wherein have we robbed thee? In tithes and offerings."*

And <u>**Matthew 23:23**</u>, *"Woe unto you, scribes and Pharisees, hypocrites! for ye pay tithe of mint and anise and cummin, and have omitted the weightier matters of the law, judgment, mercy, and faith: these ought ye to have done, and not to leave the other undone."*

Elohim expected them to tithe or it would be a debt, but they were also to do it with the correct attitude in place. The correct attitude for giving tithes and offerings. Judgement, mercy and faith = Righteousness, love and trust (**Matthew 23:23**).

Economically — It is an investment: **Matthew 6:20**, *"But lay up for yourselves treasures in heaven, where neither moth nor rust doth corrupt, and where thieves do not break through nor steal:"* (also see **Luke 6:38**).

Spiritually It is a blessing: **Galatians 3:9**, *"So then they which be of faith are blessed with faithful Abraham."* (**Malachi 3:10**).

Reasons for tithing

1. It is the will of Elohim (**Leviticus 27:30, Malachi 3:7-10**).

2. It is Elohim's way of blessing us and protecting our goods (**Malachi 3:10-12; Deuteronomy 14:22-29**).

3. It is Elohim's way of maintaining His servants financially, so that they can concentrate their efforts on the study and ministry of the Word.

Numbers 18:20-24, *"And the Lord spake unto Aaron, Thou shalt have no inheritance in their land, neither shalt thou have any part among them: I am thy part and thine inheritance among the children of Israel. And, behold, I have given the children of Levi all the tenth in Israel for an inheritance, for their service which they serve, even the service of the tabernacle of the congregation. Neither must the children of Israel henceforth come nigh the tabernacle of the congregation, lest they bear sin, and die.*

But the Levites shall do the service of the tabernacle of the congregation, and they shall bear their iniquity: it shall be a statute for ever throughout your generations, that among the children of Israel they have no inheritance.

But the tithes of the children of Israel, which they offer as an heave offering unto the Lord, I have given to the Levites to inherit: therefore I have said unto them, Among the children of Israel they shall have no inheritance."

Tithing demonstrates trust in Elohim as our provider, and a genuine desire to see His kingdom established.

Deuteronomy 8:18, "But thou shalt remember the Lord thy God: for it is he that giveth thee power to get wealth, that he may establish his covenant which he sware unto thy fathers, as it is this day".

Tithing is for the New Testament age also (**1 Corinthians 9:7-14, Hebrews7:1-8**).

Five reasons why some do not tithe:

1. Lack of knowledge

2. Unbelief

3. Fear

4. Greed

5. Envy

The people of Elohim were commanded to give all the tithe in **Leviticus 27:30**. Some pay tithes only on their salary income only, others pay tithes of all whether interest, bonds, rental income, or gifts etc. In the Old Testament they paid tithes of all they received whether lands, food, cattle or money.

In the New Testament, the newly formed church sold their possession they had and brought the money (tithes and offerings) to the apostles to use in the work of Elohim (**Acts 2:45 ; 4:34-35**).

Because of this the early church was instantly able to preach the Gospel to their world. Instead of waiting for a decade or two to save enough money to do so.

Now I'm not suggesting you do this, because I don't believe the church is not yet at the place where it will steward this kind of giving properly. If you do, then you may. But the responsibility remains that the members of every congregation should tithe and give offerings of all they receive as income (what comes in).

What should tithes be used for?

For the upkeep of the Ministers and needy members of the Church (Widows, the poor, orphans). Those that preach the Gospel should live by the Gospel, **1 Corinthians 9:14**, *"Even so hath the Lord ordained that they which preach the gospel should live of the gospel."* But the Ministry also must return tithes to the work of Elohim in the form of tithing into the Kingdom of Elohim.

Where should I give my tithe?

You should give your tithe at the local assembly that you attend, to the Ministry that you partake of as your local assembly (storehouse).

Elohim's plan for both the secular and spiritual world demands that a man's labour and effort bears fruit that he may have his physical needs met (**Malachi 3:8-10**). So tithes and offerings plant seeds that germinate in economic blessings.

What should I tithe out of?

We return tithes to the Lord out of all that is an increase or income (all that we receive or comes into our possession).

We should bring what Elohim requires and not what we want to bring e.g. Cain and Abel. If we really have "nothing" to give, we have time, and everyone knows time is money. So when you give 1/10th of your time to helping the work of Elohim, it won't be too long before time will turn into money.

Where Does The Tithes and Offering Go?

"And, behold, I have given the children of Levi all the tenth in Israel for an inheritance, for their service which they serve, even the service of the tabernacle of the congregation." **Numbers 18:21**.

And again, *"Even so hath the Lord ordained that they which the gospel should live of the gospel."* **1 Corinthians 9:14** . It is ordained that the tithes would go to support the ministry (people) and was to be brought into the storehouse which is Elohim's House, or the Church.

Offerings were given over and above, or apart from the tithes, as a freewill gift for the physical work of the house of Elohim e.g. fixing the building or paying bills (**Exodus 25:2,8; 35:5,20 ; 1 Chronicles 29:3,14,17 ; 2 Corinthians 8:2,12,14 ; and 9:6-7**).

Can I Pay my tithes to the needy or a charity?

The tithes are not for the needy or charity, but for the ministry. Elohim has given command to bring tithe and offerings into His house. Anything else would be robbing

Elohim. There is however an ordained ministry to help the needy and charities called Alms deed. Alms were to be given from separate individual gifts, not from the church or ministry (see **Luke 11:41**).

Alms are to be given without reward or public notice (**Matthew 6:1-4**). They are designed for the needy or those that cannot work (**Acts 3:2-3**). It is mainly a ministry of the wealthy or well off (**Acts 10:2-3**). It was sometimes a ministry of the talented, who could make things for the needy or make something for sale to buy other needed items (**Acts 9:36-39**).

Tithes, offering and the law

Tithes and offerings did not begin with the Law of Moses. Abraham did it 400 years before the Law was given (**Genesis 14:18-20; 28:11-22**).

To this day tithing is considered an act of the faith covenant through which we in the New Testament become 'children of Abraham' by faith (**Galatians 3:7**).

Some would try to get us to believe that Yahoshuah did away with tithes and offerings. On the contrary, He sanctioned it when He told the Pharisees and Sadducees that they were doing the right thing by tithing but just needed to adjust their attitude of giving of it to be acceptable to Elohim (**Matthew 23:23**).

Paul also sanctioned the giving of tithes. (**1 Corinthians 9:7-14 ; Hebrews 7:4-8**).

Tithing the tithe

Deuteronomy 26 gives us an example and pattern of how we are to return the tithe to Yah. Tithing is done with words (preferably in your prayer closet at home).

The tithe is offered to your High Priest, Yahoshuah Messiah. The model is given for us to follow so just begin to pattern it.

A Major function of tithing the tithe is that it checks backsliding by encouraging you to cleanse yourself first. You will not be able to follow the pattern of **Deuteronomy 26**, if there is sin in your life, without a pricked heart; the response at this point should be to repent.

We also need to spend some time worshiping the Lord of the tithe, and offer the tithe to Him as a sweet sacrifice. Then and only then can the blessing be released.

Deuteronomy 26:5-10, *"And thou shalt speak and say before the Lord thy God, A Syrian ready to perish was my father, and he went down into Egypt, and sojourned there with a few, and became there a nation, great, mighty, and populous: And the Egyptians evil entreated us, and afflicted us, and laid upon us hard bondage: And when we cried unto the Lord God of our fathers, the Lord heard our voice, and looked on our affliction, and our labour, and our oppression:*

And the Lord brought us forth out of Egypt with a mighty hand, and with an outstretched arm, and with great terribleness, and with signs, and with wonders: And he hath brought us into this place, and hath given us this land, even a land that floweth with milk and honey. And now, behold, I have brought the firstfruits of the land, which thou, O Lord, hast given me. And thou shalt set it before the Lord thy

God, and worship before the Lord thy God:"

Confess your sins

1. Thank Him for deliverance from all your enemies and problems (name them).

2. Praise Him for the specific blessings He has given to you.

3. Recognise the opportunity to bring your first fruits that He has given to you.

4. Worship Him and give your gift.

Signposts of poverty

1. Refusing instruction (**Proverbs 13:18; Deuteronomy 28:45-48; Deuteronomy 28:1-2**).

2. Following vain persons (**Proverbs 28:19, Matthew 18:19**).

3. Withholding more than you should or being mean (**Proverbs 11:24; 2 Corinthians 9:6**).

4. Motivation to get rich for self (**Deuteronomy 8:11-18**).

5. Neglecting the material needs of the work of Elohim (**Haggai 1:2-9; Matthew 6:33**).

6. Disunity (**Ecclesiastes 4:8-12**).

7. Laziness (**Proverbs 10:4-5**).

To understand the poverty strategy of Satan, it must first be understood that the people are the "Church". So when Church people are attacked by the forces of fear, doubt and unbelief in their personal lives, and the assembly begins to show the above sign posts by taking on those attitudes and characteristics, it will lead to the following kind of thinking:

- People can't give what they don't have

- People won't have what they don't have the means to get.

- People can't give what they fear they will not be able to replace

The end result of this is that the people and the assembly suffer financially. When the church suffers financially; then the spreading of the Gospel suffers also.

Yet prosperity is promised to the HEBREW BELIEVER and is part of Elohim's highest declared will (**3 John 2; Joshua 1:7-8; Psalm 1:3; Nehemiah 2:20; Ezra 6:14; 2 Chronicles 20:20, Philippians 4:19, 2Cor 8:9, Deuteronomy 28:16, 8,11-13**).

Breaking the poverty cycle

1. Put poverty in its rightful position (**Ephesians 1:22-23, Matthew 6:33, Matthew 16:25**). Get your priorities right.

2. Put the kingdom of Elohim first. Give your tithes and offerings to Elohim with a correct attitude, and be faithful so that Elohim can bless you the way He wants to.

3. Acknowledge the source of your blessings (**Malachi 3:7-8, Deuteronomy 8:18, Proverbs 3:9**). Many have come under the curse, because they have forgotten who gave them what they have.

4. Put feet to your faith — In Deuteronomy 8:18, the word "power" means "ability" and that includes ideas, skills and energy. You have your part to play. Ideas x ability x work = reward. It is Elohim that gives us ideas, and that is true wealth. **Proverbs 8:12**, *"I wisdom dwell with prudence, and find out knowledge of witty inventions."*

5. Look beyond present circumstances (**Proverbs 29:18, Romans 4:17-21**).

6. Put your hands to the plough and set the ideas to work, **Psalm 1:3**. Set about improving what you already do; do it more efficiently.

7. Be Messiah centered in your faith continually. Let the Bible be your ultimate and final authority on all questions. Have you caught your Pastor's vision for the future?

   Do you have a well-balanced view of prosperity? Do you consider Yahoshuah to be Lord of everything you have? Do you show the love of Elohim by your actions toward the brethren? Do you lead a continuously Spirit led and Spirit filled life? (**Palms 92:13, Luke 6:38, Psalm 119:128**).

Summary

A legal giver gives because the Law (Bible) says so. A legal giver gives because he has to. A loving giver gives because he wants to not because he is forced.

Give of yourself - your time, talents and treasury. Give it all to Yahoshuah and the Lord will give it back to you. **Luke 6:38 : Galatians 6:7.**

The search your bible section — Fit appropriate scripture to the matching questions.

1. When we give, what measure will we receive?

2. For what purpose did Messiah become poor?

3. What kind of person does Elohim love?

4. If we would reap bountifully, what must we do first?

5. In what does the Lord take pleasure?

6. Israel robbed Elohim in two ways, with what result?

7. How did Elohim tell Israel to prove Him?

8. What was the reason for Joseph's prosperity?

9. Who lived by the tithe?

10. What must a person do to have good success and prosper?

2 Corinthians 8:9, Psalm 35:27, Numbers 18:20-24, Malachi 3:8-9, Luke 6:38, Genesis 39:2, 23, Malachi 3:10, 2 Corinthians 9:7, Joshua 1:7-8, 2 Corinthians 9:6.

Discussion

1. What are your observations about people who give generously?

2. What is the meaning of tithing and what are offerings?

3. Compare the impoverished in a congregation and those that prosper and do you notice any commonalities among the impoverished?

4. What should those who don't tithe do?

5. What can the impoverished do about their situation right now to change it?

6. What sticks out in the lesson for you?

Chapter Thirteen

HOLINESS

Part 1 - Principles of holiness

Introduction

The meaning of the root word "holy" is to be separated or withdrawn from that which is common or unclean, and be consecrated to what is sacred and pure. Elohim alone is pure and holy. He is perfect; man is imperfect. He is divine; man is human. His is morally perfect; man is sinful.

So it is Elohim abhors that which is sin is clear to all who know Him. It is easy so understand that He cannot tolerate sin of any kind. You can misunderstand His mercy to mean tolerance of sin, but to Him it is vile and revolting. Therefore, it is evident that man must become holy in order to have fellowship with Elohim.

Holiness is a condition of the heart. It is a the sum total of our attitudes and motives as we strive to draw closer to Elohim. Yahoshuah said, "Blessed are the pure in heart for they shall see God..." Our hearts are not really pure, or we would not do the things we do. What makes us acceptable is when our talents, skills, gifts, motives and mind are separated and dedicated to the service of Elohim. Then He can really use us and in the process separate us for His Kingdom.

To sanctify means to separate from evil and dedicate exclusively to the service of Elohim. Man's part is to bring himself to the sanctifying influence of the Holy Ghost and allow Elohim to work his will. Sinful man is wholly incapable of making himself holy. This can only happen through the work of the Holy Ghost.

There is nothing man can do to merit sanctification. All man's efforts are as filthy rags.

The Holy one is happy to sanctify and cleanse us. The process of sanctification begins the moment a person hears or reads the gospel message, for the Word of Elohim has a cleansing influence in the heart of the hearer **John 15:3, John 17:17**.

There is a definite power in Elohim's Word to convict a sinner or sinning saint of their sins and reveal to them their need of a closer walk with Elohim.

This will allow sanctification and deeper consecration of themselves. It is therefore the responsibility of every Elohim fearing believer to see to it that they keep themselves under the influence of the Spirit of Elohim by repentance, surrender to His will, consecration, dedication, separation from the world, faith and obedience to His Word.

Since none of us are born perfect, the purpose of our Walk here on earth is to be perfected (matured) in Christ (**2 Peter 3:18**).

The believer who is filled with the Spirit of Elohim, walks after the Spirit, is led by the Spirit and dedicates themselves to live a holy life.

One that purposes to do the will of Elohim, live a life above sin and feels no condemnation.

There are many advantages and rewards of holy living. The first is that the believer will enjoy happiness, His life will be more fruitful and fulfilling, more satisfying, for it will be a life of service to Elohim and others.

Holiness is in essence the very nature of Elohim. Elohim is Holy **Leviticus 19:2**, *"Speak unto all the congregation of the children of Israel, and say unto them, Ye shall be holy: for I the Lord your God am holy;"* (also see **Leviticus 20:7**).

This is essentially the doctrine of Sanctification. Elohim is Holy in Himself (**Leviticus 19:2; 20:7**) Holiness is the very nature of Elohim.

To truly understand holiness, we must understand that every attribute of Elohim stems from what Elohim is; Elohim is Love **1 John 4:8**, *"He that loveth not knoweth not God; for God is love."* and Elohim is holy.

The essence of all that is called holiness is contained in the principle of love, because true holiness is motivated by love; (Matthew 22:26-40; Mark; 12:28-31; Romans 13:8-10).

So if we love our neighbour as ourselves, we will not kill them, steal their husband or wife, nor insight lust knowingly. The Bible teaches that holiness and love are synonymous (the same).

2 Chronicles 20:21, *"And when he had consulted with the people, he appointed singers unto the Lord, and that should praise the beauty of holiness, as they went out before the army, and to say, Praise the Lord; for his mercy endureth for ever."* When they praised Elohim's holiness, they actually praised him for his 'mercy' or love.

Sin which is all wrongdoing, is an attack on Elohim's holiness or Elohim Himself, so sin is an offence against Elohim personally Psalm 51:4, *"Against thee, thee only, have I sinned, and done this evil in thy sight: that thou mightest be justified when thou speakest, and be clear when thou judgest."*

The most basic definition of holiness is to be separate or different. Holiness is the idea of separation, consecration, devotion to the service of Elohim above anything else. It is sharing in Elohim's purity and abstaining from defilement by the world. Holiness is both a state of being as well as a process that must be worked out in the Believer's life. As a Christian you are commanded to be holy and through Elohim you become holy it's a work of grace.

Holiness means loving what Elohim loves, hating what Elohim hates and acting as Messiah would have acted in every situation. When we say Elohim is holy, we are also saying He is sanctified. We are all to be holy or sanctified — (**Ephesians 1:4; 5:27**); **Colossians 1:22**, *"In the body of his flesh through death, to present you holy and unblameable and unreproveable in his sight:"*

Righteousness is different from holiness. It is a gift from Elohim to man of the legal right to stand in His presence without guilt or shame as a result of what Yahoshuah did on our behalf. Holiness is a process which begins when a person is Born again and continues for the duration of their Christian life.

Holiness requires personal effort on the part of the individual. A person can be more holy or less holy, but all can only be either right with Elohim (righteous) or in sin (unrighteous). The remedy to sin is therefore always repentance **1 John 1:9**, *"If we confess our sins, he is faithful and just to forgive us our sins, and to cleanse us from all unrighteousness."* (**Acts 3:19**).

There is a definite process by which Elohim works His holiness into us — **Philippians 2:12-13**, *"Wherefore, my beloved, as ye have always obeyed, not as in my presence only, but now much more in my absence, work out your own salvation with fear and trembling. For it is God which worketh in you both to will and to do of his good pleasure."*

Holiness is a partnership or joint venture which we can't implement without Him and He won't do it without our involvement also. It takes the Holy Spirit and a committed believer working together to produce a holy life. The process of Holiness involves both the inner and outer man.

1 Corinthians 6:19-20, *"What? know ye not that your body is the temple of the Holy Ghost which is in you, which ye* have of God, and ye are not your own? For ye are bought with a price: therefore glorify God in your body, and in your spirit, which are God's." (**1 Thessalonians 5:23**). Some religious people stress outward forms of holiness (**Matthew 23:27**). Others profess inward holiness.

The Bible teaches holiness always begins on the inside and manifests itself on the outside. Outward forms of holiness do not guarantee a change on the inside, but a change on the inside is always confirmed on the outside.

Proverbs 23:7, *"For as he thinketh in his heart, so is he: Eat and drink, saith he to thee; but his heart is not with thee."* The Bible teaches that we are to dedicate ourselves to the pursuit of holiness, by cleansing ourselves from the filthiness of both the flesh (outward lifestyle) and the spirit (inner thought and attitude life).

2 Corinthians 7:1, *"Having therefore these promises, dearly beloved, let us cleanse ourselves from all filthiness of the flesh and spirit, perfecting holiness in the fear of God."*

Five basic principles that govern holiness

The principle of imitation requires that I ask, What would Yahoshuah do in this situation? **Ephesians 5:1** *"Be ye therefore followers of Elohim, as dear children;"* Imitating Elohim means thinking, speaking and behaving like Him in every situation or decision and patterning Him as closely as possible.

The principle of the golden rule requires that we aim and seek to work to the highest standards is by asking, what would I have liked someone else to do to me? **Matthew 7:12** *"Therefore all things whatsoever ye would that men should* *do to you, do ye even so to them: for this is the law and the prophets."*

The third principle is the principle of reflected glory This principle asks, does this situation, thing, behaviour or conversation bring glory to Elohim? **1 Corinthians 10:31** *"Whether therefore ye eat, or drink, or whatsoever ye do, do all to the glory of God"*.

The principle of thanksgiving found in **Colossians 3:17** says, *"And whatsoever ye do in word or deed, do all in the name of the Lord Jesus, giving thanks to God and the Father by him"*.

We must be mindful to ask if we can be involved with this activity or conversation and say thank you to Elohim that we dressed that way, spoke that way or behaved that way.

The combination principle in action - *"Whether therefore ye eat, or drink, or whatsoever ye do, do all to the glory of Elohim"* **1 Corinthians 10:31**. "

And whatsoever ye do in word or deed, do all in the name of the Yah Jesus, giving thanks to Elohim and the Father by him" **Colossians 3:17**.

Notice the "Whatsoever", this means if you have some clothes that don't give glory to Elohim; or if you are in a situation or place where you can't shout, "Thank you Jesus I give you the Glory", then you ought not to be there, wear it or do it.

Ask yourself, "Will this give glory to Elohim and can I say thank you Jesus for, with a free conscience and a true heart"? If not I would advise you to leave well alone and do what you know glorifies Elohim.

Part 2 - Holiness on the inside

This scripture opens up that holiness is the product of dealing with our inner dimension of spirit life so that the external aspects of our lives begin to transform. It is not outward activity that changes our inner world, but our inner decisions that change our outer world and activity.

The most basic definition of 'holiness' is 'separate' or be different. Holiness is fundamentally the idea of separation, consecration, devotion to the service of God, sharing in Elohim's purity and abstaining from defilement by the world. For the believer is separated from the world unto Elohim.

This is both a state of being and standing for Elohim, as well as a process being worked out in the believer's life. As a Christian you are to be holy and through Elohim you're becoming holy. Holiness means loving what Elohim loves, hating what Elohim hates and acting as Messiah would have acted in every situation.

Another word for holiness is sanctification, 1 **Peter 1:14-16**, *"As obedient children, not fashioning yourselves according to the former lusts in your ignorance: But as he which hath called you is holy, so be ye holy in all manner of* *conversation; Because it is written, Be ye holy; for I am holy."* and we are commanded to be holy or sanctified, (**Leviticus 20:7; Ephesians 1:4; 5:27; Colossians 1:22**).

Righteousness is different from holiness and they should not be confused. Righteousness is a gift from Elohim to man of the legal right to stand in his presence without guilt or shame as a result of receiving Jesus as Yah and Saviour.

Holiness is a process which begins when a person is Born again, and continues for the duration of the Christian life, Holiness requires effort on the part of the individual, but righteousness is a gift.

A person may become more holy or less holy, but all can only either be right with Elohim (righteous) or in sin (unrighteous), not righteous and more righteous.

The remedy for unrighteousness is repentance from sin (**1 John 1:9**); **Acts 3:19**, *"Repent ye therefore, and be converted, that your sins may be blotted out, when the times of refreshing shall come from the presence of the Lord."*

Sin is basically an attack on Elohim's holiness or Elohim himself, so sin is an offence against Elohim personally and must be addressed by the individual in repentance (**Psalm 51:4**).

Belonging to Elohim means being like him or imitating him. So because Elohim is holy, we are to be holy. This requires that we deal with sin by repentance and be separated from our old life unto Elohim through love and service.

The pursuit of holiness

The Bible teaches that we are to dedicate ourselves to the pursuit of holiness, by cleansing ourselves from the filthiness of both the flesh (outer-man), and the spirit (inner-man) **2 Corinthians 7:1.**

Draw near to Elohim: He says in His Word found in **James 4:8**, *"Draw nigh to God, and he will draw nigh to you. Cleanse your hands, ye sinners; and purify your hearts, ye double minded."*

Renew your mind with the Word of Elohim, **Romans 12:2**, *"And be not conformed to this world: but be ye transformed by the renewing of your mind, that ye may prove what is that good, and acceptable, and perfect, will of God."*

Convict your emotions: **John 16:7-8**, *"Nevertheless I tell you the truth; It is expedient for you that I go away: for if I go not away, the Comforter will not come unto you; but if I depart, I will send him unto you. And when he is come, he will reprove the world of sin, and of righteousness, and of judgment:"* Empower your will, **Galatians 5:16**, *"This I say then, Walk in the Spirit, and ye shall not fulfil the lust of the flesh."*

Provide way of escape **1 Corinthians 10:13**, *"There hath no temptation taken you but such as is common to man: but God is faithful, who will not suffer you to be tempted above that ye are able; but will with the temptation also make a way to escape, that ye may be able to bear it."*

Cause us to triumph **2 Corinthians 2:14**, *"Now thanks be unto God, which always causeth us to triumph in Christ, and maketh manifest the savour of his knowledge by us in every* place."

Present our bodies, **Romans 12:1**, *"I beseech you therefore, brethren, by the mercies of God, that ye present your bodies a living sacrifice, holy, acceptable unto God, which is your reasonable service."*

Meditate on scripture **Joshua 1:8**, *"This book of the law shall not depart out of thy mouth; but thou shalt meditate therein day and night, that thou mayest observe to do according to all that is written therein: for then thou shalt make thy way prosperous, and then thou shalt have good success."*

Set our affections, **Colossians 3:2**, *"Set your affection on things above, not on things on the earth."*

Submit your will, **James 4:7**, *"Submit yourselves therefore to God. Resist the devil, and he will flee from you."*

Flee temptation, **1 Timothy 6:11**, *"But thou, O man of God, flee these things; and follow after righteousness, godliness, faith, love, patience, meekness."*

And again **2 Timothy 2:22-24**, *"Flee also youthful lusts: but follow righteousness, faith, charity, peace, with them that call on the Lord out of a pure heart. But foolish and unlearned questions avoid, knowing that they do gender strifes. And the servant of the Lord must not strive; but be gentle unto all men, apt to teach, patient,"*

Resist the devil, (see **James 4:7** above).

PRACTICAL HOLINESS

Attitudes	Galatians 5:19-21," Now the works of the flesh are manifest, which are these; Adultery, fornication, uncleanness, lasciviousness, Idolatry, witchcraft, hatred, variance, emulations, wrath, strife, seditions, heresies, Envyings, murders, drunkenness, revellings, and such like: of the which I tell you before, as I have also told you in time past, that they which do such things shall not inherit the kingdom of God."
	Ephesians 4:31-32, "Let all bitterness, and wrath, and anger, and clamour, and evil speaking, be put away from you, with all malice: And be ye kind one to another, tenderhearted, forgiving one another, even as God for Christ's sake hath forgiven you."
	Either you have Elohim's attitudes or you have your own. The wrong attitudes will lead us to sin and ultimately to hell.

The tongue	James 1:26, "If any man among you seem to be religious, and bridleth not his tongue, but deceiveth his own heart, this man's religion is vain." (also James 3:1-12) James 4:11, "Speak not evil one of another, brethren. He that speaketh evil of his brother, and judgeth his brother, speaketh evil of the law, and judgeth the law: but if thou judge the law, thou art not a doer of the law, but a judge." James 5:12, "But above all things, my brethren, swear not, neither by heaven, neither by the earth, neither by any other oath: but let your yea be yea; and your nay, nay; lest ye fall into condemnation." Proverbs 18:21, "Death and life are in the power of the tongue: and they that love it shall eat the fruit thereof." Since life and death are in the words we speak, we can kill many things in our life that should live and visa-versa. Ultimately we may shorten our lives due to lack of self-control.

Adornment and dress	Deuteronomy 22:5, "The woman shall not wear that which pertaineth unto a man, neither shall a man put on a woman's garment: for all that do so are abomination unto the LORD thy God."
What all of the above combine to say, is that we should dress simply and not ostentatiously. We should dress according to our gender, speak like our gender, behave like our gender and wear our hair like our gender. To do anything else causes gender confusion and ultimately leads to sins that may never even have been intended.	1 Timothy 2:9; In like manner also, that women adorn themselves in modest apparel, with shamefacedness and sobriety; not with broided hair, or gold, or pearls, or costly array; **1 Peter 3:3-4**,. *Whose adorning let it not be that outward adorning of plaiting the hair, and of wearing of gold, or of putting on of apparel; But let it be the hidden man of the heart, in that which is not corruptible, even the ornament of a meek and quiet spirit, which is in the sight of God of great price."* (**Isaiah 3:16-26 & 4:1**) **1 Corinthians 11:14-15**, *"Doth not even nature itself teach you, that, if a man have long hair, it is a shame unto him? But if a woman have long hair, it is a glory to her: for her hair is given her for a covering."*

The thoughts	Philippians 4:8, *"Finally, brethren, whatsoever things are true, whatsoever things are honest, whatsoever things are just, whatsoever things are pure, whatsoever things are lovely, whatsoever things are of good report; if there be any virtue, and if there be any praise, think on these things."*
	Proverbs 23:7, *"For as he thinketh in his heart, so is he: Eat and drink, saith he to thee; but his heart is not with thee."*
	2 Corinthians 10:5, *"Casting down imaginations, and every high thing that exalteth itself against the knowledge of God, and bringing into captivity every thought to the obedience of Christ;"*
	Once again, either we control our thought life or our thoughts control us. If we lose control of our thoughts, ultimately we lose control of our minds and will end up controlled by someone or something else and be led to hell.
Respect for human life Life is special, it doesn't matter whose. We are to nurture life, respect life and preserve life.	Exodus 20:13, *"Thou shalt not kill."* Matthew 5:44, *"But I say unto you, Love your enemies, bless them that curse you, do good to them that hate you, and pray for them which despitefully use you, and persecute you;"* 1 John 3:15 *"Whosoever hateth his brother is a murderer: and ye know that no murderer hath eternal life abiding in him"*

Sexual Relationships	
The proper context for sexual relationships according to our Elohim is between a man and woman married to each other. Attempts to read the texts against unlawful sex as anything other than prohibitions of fornication, adultery and homosexual behaviour will not ultimately work. Unlawful sexual relationships are not sanctioned).	**Genesis 1:27, 31**, *"So God created man in his own image, in the image of God created he him; male and female created he them.* **Verse 31,** *"And God saw every thing that he had made, and, behold, it was very good. And the evening and the morning were the sixth day."* **Genesis 2:24**, *"Therefore shall a man leave his father and his mother, and shall cleave unto his wife: and they shall be one flesh."* **Proverbs 5:18-19**, *"Let thy fountain be blessed: and rejoice with the wife of thy youth. Let her be as the loving hind and pleasant roe; let her breasts satisfy thee at all times; and be thou ravished always with her love."* **1 Corinthians 7:3**, *"Let the husband render unto the wife due benevolence: and likewise also the wife unto the husband."* **Hebrews 13:4**, *"Marriage is honourable in all, and the bed undefiled: but whoremongers and adulterers God will judge."* **(Leviticus 18 ; Leviticus 20:13; Romans 1:18-32; 1 Corinthians 6:9-10; 1 Timothy 1:8-10):**

Prejudice

Although you may indeed be a Hebrew, that does not make you a judge or better than others nor give you the right to be prejudiced. You were chosen not because of anything in you, but because of Grace. Your true role now is to be a light to attract others to your Elohim, so remember that.

Acts 10:34, *"Then Peter opened his mouth, and said, Of a truth I perceive that God is no respecter of persons:"*

Romans 2:11, *"For there is no respect of persons with God"*

Galatians 3:28, *"There is neither Jew nor Greek, there is neither bond nor free, there is neither male nor female: for ye are all one in Christ Jesus."*

1 Timothy 5:21, *"I charge thee before God, and the Lord Jesus Christ, and the elect angels, that thou observe these things without preferring one before another, doing nothing by partiality."*

The eye	**Psalm 101:3**, *"I will set no wicked thing before mine eyes: I hate the work of them that turn aside; it shall not cleave to me."* **Psalm 119:37**, *"Turn away mine eyes from beholding vanity; and quicken thou me in thy way."* Matt 6:22,23 Lack of control over our eyes can also lead us to sin and ultimately to hell. Yahoshuah said we can look at a woman with lust in our hearts and at that point we already sinned. Its because what we see or envision becomes our future.
Stewardship of the body	**1 Corinthians 3:16-17,** "Know ye not that ye are the temple of God, and that the Spirit of God dwelleth in you? If any man defile the temple of God, him shall God destroy; for the temple of God is holy, which temple ye are" **(1 Corinthians 6:12, 19-20).** **Colossians 3:5,** "Mortify therefore your members which are upon the earth; fornication, uncleanness, inordinate affection, evil concupiscence, and covetousness, which is idolatry:" Because we are Elohim's temple there are certain sins that should never occur in our bodies because they show a blatant disrespect for our bodies. This should be dealt with by mortification of the flesh nature.

Practical Tips

1. Establish a habit of prayer at set times it will help you to become disciplined.

2. Settle in a habit of systematic bible study at set times it will do the same as above.

3. Consolidate a habit of going to church as often as possible missing no meetings where it can possibly be helped it will develop an attendance habit that will help you throughout all of your spiritual walk.

4. Learn to ponder Elohim's word by memorising and reciting key verses, chapters, or books of the Bible, beginning with salvation (Acts 2:38, John 3:5, Mark 16:15-20, Luke 24: 44-49).

5. Reduce the amount of time you spend in front of the T.V. computer games or any other distracting influence and spend it with Elohim through praying, witnessing and bible study instead.

6. Be obedient to Pastoral and church leadership, even when you can't see what they can as long as following them doesn't lead to sinning against Elohim.

7. If you have a problem spiritual or personal you can't handle or share with anyone else, share it with your Pastor. He is there to help and counsel you. If the problem is with your pastor, share it with one of the older church mothers and take advice.

Part 3 - Practical holiness

Introduction

Holiness has an external or practical dimension that has to be addressed. For while Yah judges the heart, people see the outward actions, dress, adornment and other things that either draw or repel them concerning our Elohim.

We must therefore be conscious of what we do, say and project to others. For man looks on the outward appearance of any and every situation and makes a decision based on what they see or experience.

So in this lesson, we will take a look at some issues that people consider to be issues of holiness or at very least contention that need to be understood in the context of scripture so as to bring glory to Elohim.

Practical holiness requires self-control of every aspect of the human environment and lifestyle. We must therefore be watchful as to what we believe, think, say, do, look at etc.

Secrets to successful holy living

1. Allow the power of the Holy Ghost to teach and change you.

2. Allow Yah to teach you how to pray and how to communicate better since it's through Him that we grow.

3. Find the mind of Elohim realising that it is only after you surrender your will to Elohim's will that you will know peace.

4. Read your Bible daily and let it come alive in your heart. Attend Bible study, listen to good preaching. Think about the messages and ask questions that will clarify doctrine.

5. Dedicate yourself fully to Elohim's service and will. Don't be side-tracked, keep His will as your top priority.

6. Live each day one day at a time and repair any damage that would separate you from Elohim quickly so that you can keep moving in the direction of getting closer to Elohim.

7. Keep your eyes off the faults of others and on Yahoshuah the one who has the answer to every problem.

8. Witness of the hope that is within you and watch your

life be more victorious because of the power of Elohim upon you.

9. Discuss your problems with your pastor.

Physical principles of holiness

God has a standard of holiness - There was no need for a standard until sin arrived. The moment sin arrived, they were changed forever. **Genesis 3:7, 21**, *"And the eyes of them both were opened, and they knew that they were naked; and they sewed fig leaves together, and made themselves aprons."* And **verse 21** *"Unto Adam also and to his wife did the Lord God make coats of skins, and clothed them."*

Nakedness today is demon inspired - What causes a man or woman to dress in less and less clothing is more than likely a demon of lust. **Mark 5:15**, *"And they come to Jesus, and see him that was possessed with the devil, and had the legion, sitting, and clothed, and in his right mind: and they were afraid."*

After Yahoshuah cast the devil out of the man, the first thing it mentions is that he put on clothes and was in his right mind. This suggests that those who are naked are not acting out of their right mind (In **Exodus 32:25-28**) Moses saw the people naked and took a stand against it by killing those who were "dressed naked" (as good as naked).

In **1 Samuel 19:24**, Saul takes off his clothes and lays naked before all and got up and preached afterwards. Later this same man would end up going into witchcraft. This is because nakedness and witchcraft have always gone hand in hand.

Clothing should be modest - The Bible teaches that Christians aught to dress modestly.

1 Timothy 2:9, *"In like manner also, that women adorn themselves in modest apparel, with shamefacedness and sobriety; not with broided hair, or gold, or pearls, or costly array;"* and **1Peter 3:3**, *"Whose adorning let it not be that outward adorning of plaiting the hair, and of* wearing of gold, or of putting on of apparel".

The Greek word for "shamefaced" means modesty. The Bible therefore teaches that Christian modesty doesn't worldly cosmetics or worldly dress, it leads to balanced presentation that doesn't aim to stir up lust e.g. as in the attire of an harlot (**Proverbs 7:10**).

The world believes beauty comes from dressing up the flesh with stones, jewels, and worldly lust generating cloths. The Bible teaches that true beauty comes from character and right behaviour from th3e heart.

This is the argument of (**1 Timothy 2:9 and 1 Peter 3:3**). This doesn't mean you don't take care of your body or present yourself looking your best, but that this is not where you place priority and emphasis.

The wearing of Jewelry is to be discouraged, **Genesis 35:2-4**, *"Then Jacob said unto his household, and to all that were with him, Put away the strange gods that are among you, and be clean, and change your garments: And let us arise, and go up to Bethel; and I will make there an altar unto God, who answered me in the day of my distress, and was with me in the way which I went.*

And they gave unto Jacob all the strange gods which were in their hand, and all their earrings which were in their ears; and Jacob hid them under the oak which was by Shechem."

And **Exodus 33:4-6**, *"And when the people heard these evil tidings, they mourned: and no man did put on him his ornaments. For the Lord had said unto Moses, Say unto the children of Israel, Ye are a stiffnecked people: I will come up into the midst of thee in a moment, and consume thee: therefore now put off thy ornaments from thee, that I may know what to do unto thee. And the children of Israel stripped themselves of their ornaments by the mount Horeb."*

The above scriptures are important, because in them we find Elohim commanding His people to put off their adornment. We also find that each time Israel fell into idolatry they instantly wore jewelry and heathen attire.

I have always found it interesting that each time people backslide from the faith, when I next met them, it was interesting that they were fully decked down in jewelry, make up and heathen attire.

It is further interesting that the scripture points out that they formed, "god(s)" from their jewelry that they brought out of Egypt. The origin of jewelry has always been based in idolatry. The adorning of the body with jewels is originally associated with self-deification or the making of false gods.

The Encyclopaedia Britannic, 1973 Vol.12 p 1030 says, "The wearing of stone and metal ornaments had its origin in idolatry, witchcraft, superstition and vanity". Notice the following verses from **2 Kings 9:22, 30**, *"And it came to pass, when Joram saw Jehu, that he said, Is it peace, Jehu?*

And he answered, What peace, so long as the whoredoms of thy mother Jezebel and her witchcrafts are so many?" And **Verse 30**, *"And when Jehu was come to Jezreel, Jezebel heard of it; and she painted her face, and tired her head, and looked out at a window."*

Jezabel who is the mother of whoredoms and condemned for her witchcraft was a woman who disguised her appearance to dress like a harlot or prostitute.

So what is the origin of make up? The use of eye make up which enhances sexual appeal was founded in Egypt in 3500 BC according to Encyclopedia Britannic 1984 Vol. 5 p. 196.

Spiritually Egypt is the place of bondage and slavery **Exodus 20:2**, *"I am the Lord thy God, which have brought thee out of the land of Egypt, out of the house of bondage"*

Encyclopedia Britannic 1973 Vol. 6 p. 566, "Until recently all religious groups did take a stand on this issue: "Until world war 1, make up was considered improper and even immoral" Americana Encyclopedia Britannica 1984 Vol. 8 p 34, "During the early Christian era, cosmetics disappeared to Europe".

From a treasurer of early Christianity by Anne Fremantle; She wrote, Tertullian's (one of the early church fathers) view on make-up was; "You must not overstep the line to which simple and sufficient elegance limits its desires which is pleasing to God."

And "Against Him those women sin, who torment their skin with potions, stain their cheeks with rouge, and extend the line of their eyes with black colouring. Doubtless, they are dissatisfied with God's plastic skill.

Take not to yourself such robes and garments as play the role of pimp or pander. Let us cast away earthly ornaments, if we desire heavenly." This was the Church's view 300 years after Pentecost.

Some special modern day issues

A. Head covering and hair

1. You have a natural covering which is your hair.

2. There is another covering which is culturally determined (hat, veil etc).

3. Nature takes precedence over culture but we are to be aware of cultural differences and respect enough to dress culturally appropriately when we are in someone else's space.

4. Men ought to have their heads uncovered and women covered (This means men – hair should be cut. Women - uncut).

5. Whether covered or uncovered, it's determined by you wearing your hair in a gender appropriate way.

1 Corinthians 11:3-16, *"But I would have you know, that the head of every man is Christ; and the head of the woman is the man; and the head of Christ is God. Every man praying or prophesying, having his head covered, dishonoureth his head. But every woman that prayeth or prophesieth with her head uncovered dishonoureth her head: for that is even all one as if she were shaven.*

For if the woman be not covered, let her also be shorn: but if it be a shame for a woman to be shorn or shaven, let her be covered. For a man indeed ought not to cover his head, forasmuch as he is the image and glory of God: but the woman is the glory of the man.

For the man is not of the woman: but the woman of the man. Neither was the man created for the woman; but the woman for the man. For this cause ought the woman to have power on her head because of the angels.

Nevertheless neither is the man without the woman, neither the woman without the man, in the Lord. For as the woman is of the man, even so is the man also by the woman; but all things of God. Judge in yourselves: is it comely that a woman pray unto God uncovered?

Doth not even nature itself teach you, that, if a man have long hair, it is a shame unto him? But if a woman have long hair, it is a glory to her: for her hair is given her for a covering. But if any man seem to be contentious, we have no such custom, neither the churches of God."

B. Sabbath keeping and the law

The Sabbath is a part of the law. There is only one law though many try to divide it up. **Numbers 15:29**, *"Ye shall have one law for him that sinneth through ignorance, both for him that is born among the children of Israel, and for the stranger that sojourneth among them."*

The law has been abolished or done-away-with so it's no longer in force in New Testament times.

2 Corinthians 3:3-17, *"Forasmuch as ye are manifestly declared to be the epistle of Christ ministered by us, written not with ink, but with the Spirit of the living God; not in tables of stone, but in fleshy tables of the heart. And such*

326

trust have we through Christ to God-ward: Not that we are sufficient of ourselves to think any thing as of ourselves; but our sufficiency is of God; Who also hath made us able ministers of the new testament; not of the letter, but of the spirit: for the letter killeth, but the spirit giveth life.

But if the ministration of death, written and engraven in stones, was glorious, so that the children of Israel could not stedfastly behold the face of Moses for the glory of his countenance; which glory was to be done away:

How shall not the ministration of the spirit be rather glorious? For if the ministration of condemnation be glory, much more doth the ministration of righteousness exceed in glory. For even that which was made glorious had no glory in this respect, by reason of the glory that excelleth.

For if that which is done away was glorious, much more that which remaineth is glorious. Seeing then that we have such hope, we use great plainness of speech: And not as Moses, which put a veil over his face, that the children of Israel could not stedfastly look to the end of that which is abolished: But their minds were blinded: for until this day remaineth the same vail untaken away in the reading of the old testament; which vail is done away in Christ.

But even unto this day, when Moses is read, the vail is upon their heart. Nevertheless when it shall turn to the Lord, the vail shall be taken away. Now the Lord is that Spirit: and where the Spirit of the Lord is, there is liberty."

(Ephesians 2:15, Colossians 2:14, and Romans 10:4, Luke 16:16; Romans 7:1-7)

1. Though the law of the Sabbath is abolished, the principle of the Sabbath is not. The principle is given

in the wisdom of Elohim that we need to rest at least one day of the week.

2. When it comes to worship, we can worship every day and any day (Colossians 2:16-17).

3. Sabbath keepers are law keepers and law keepers cannot walk in grace, for either you keep the law or walk in grace (**2 Corinthians 9:14-15**).

4. Either salvation is of the law and gained by works or it's by grace and through Yahoshuah Messiah (Ephesians 2:8-9).

C. Courting and dating

The Bible is silent on the subject of dating but rich on the subject of friendship. The implication being that everybody should be friendly and that out of friendships can come relationships that lead to marriage (**Proverbs 18:24**).

1. Young people should be especially aware of lust and flee from it (**2 Timothy 2:22**).

2. Working with others in the ministry is a good way to begin to know them.

3. It is the man that seeks a wife, but it's the potential wife that signs off on the proposal. No woman should be forced to marry someone she doesn't want (**Proverbs 18:22 and Genesis 24:58**).

4. The way to choose the right person is to use your heart and your head. Listen to both, if your heart doesn't desire the person, don't marry them and if your head knows you can't work with them, don't marry them

(Romans 8:14; Galatians 5:18)

5. What is required to know that you have chosen the right person at the time, is the witness of our conscience (heart) and the Spirit (mind of Elohim). After choosing a life-mate this way, you can have a rest of faith you have chosen the very best way you could.

D. Divorce and remarriage

1. From the beginning we are charged with marrying one person for life (**Matthew 19:3-8**).

2. Whoever Elohim joins together let no one come between them (**Matthew 19:6**).

3. Due to the hardness of man's heart (unwillingness to forgive wrongs) Moses allowed divorce (**Matthew 19:8**).

4. Elohim still expects one man for one wife for one life. So polygamy is not allowed (Mark 10:9).

5. If we find a family in that way, we are to uphold the family unit but not encourage the sin. So such a man cannot become an elder (example or leader) but can be a worker (**2 Timothy 3:2**).

6. The only right we are given to divorce is that of adultery (**Matthew 19:9**).

7. So if a person divorces, it doesn't automatically give them the right to remarry, each case must be judged on its own merits.

E. Dress and adornment

1. Garments and adornment must be gender appropriate (**Deuteronomy 22:5**)

2. Garments must be modest or cover adequately (**1 Timothy 2:8-10; 1 Peter 3:3-5**).

3. Any adornment or makeup should be minimalistic in nature (modest).

F. Speech and choice of words

1. Cursing and profanity should never be in the mouth of a saint (**Ephesians 4:29**).

2. Saints should carefully weigh and choose their words (**Colossians 4:6**).

3. Only speak words that give life and avoid negative or critical words (**Proverbs 18:21**).

4. Avoid backbiting, gossip and slander of every kind (**1 Timothy 5:13; 2 Corinthians 12:20; Proverbs 11:13**).

5. When you give your word, try to keep it, if you can't keep it, signal ahead of time your inability to keep your word and what you will do to sort the situation out (**Matthew 5:37, James 5:12**).

G. Music, TV, entertainment

1. Avoid music or anything that stirs up the wrong emotions or feelings (**Proverbs 15:13**).

2. Avoid TV programmes that fall below the standards of scripture in language, images and content

(**Psalm 101:3, Job 31:1**).

3. Remember sometimes it's not the activity that's wrong, but what goes on around the activity or the nature of the entertainment.

4. Choose carefully the places you go to in order to be entertained or what happens at that place in addition to the purpose for which you attended (**Romans 12:9**).

H. Dance and sport

1. Clearly dance and sport of themselves or even theatre are not sinful in themselves, but the type of dancing matters so personal judgement must be used (**Matthew 10:28**).

2. What happens around sports and music is sometimes more important than the match or concert. The drugs and alcohol around such events is significant (**Colossians 2:8**) their minds set is not the same as ours.

I. Anything else

1. There always compromising situation for which we must use the wisdom of Elohim and the principles we have been taught.

2. One of which is the Joseph principle or run for your life – It is better to have your soul intact and leave your clothes behind than to take off your clothes and leave your soul behind. When in doubt, run for your life and sort it out afterwards (**Genesis 39:12**).

Summary

1. Holiness is a requirement for all Christians

2. Our Elohim is holy because He is separate from sin and morally pure

3. Holiness in Elohim's people refers to their separation unto Elohim and His cause.

4. When we say Christians are holy, we do not mean they are perfect, but rather that they have committed themselves to mature and be separated unto Elohim.

5. Once a person is baptised in the name of Yahoshuah (Jesus) they are washed clean from their sins, making them a temple where the Spirit of Elohim can dwell and vessel separated unto Elohim.

6. To be holy is to be spiritually minded.

7. It is impossible to be or live holy without the Holy Ghost.

8. Once we have received the Holy Ghost, we need to remain full of the Spirit so we can live a life pleasing to Elohim.

9. The opposite of holiness is worldliness and a worldly person is one whose affections are caught up in the ways of the world and not after the ways of Elohim.

10. Holiness is both internal and external in nature. Internally it's about our thoughts, attitudes and meditations. Externally it's about our speech, dress, adornment and behaviours.

11. Our activities and behaviours should reflect a godly intent in life.

12. Because our Elohim is holy and progressive, He makes all things new and takes us through a process to separate us from the world and unto Himself.

Search your bible section - Select appropriate scripture for each question

1. Is Holiness a choice or a command for a Christian?

2. Name one thing that you should present holy to Elohim.

3. What is another word for Holiness?

4. If a person entertains lustful or evil thoughts, what happens?

5. What kind of power is in the tongue?

6. What is Elohim's attitude toward lying and prostitution?

7. How does Elohim view homosexuality and prostitution?

8. Is sex outside of a monogamous marriage acceptable to Elohim?

9. Has Elohim got any favourite children?

1 Corinthians 6:9-11; Revelations 21:8; Proverbs 23:7; Romans 12:1; 1 Peter 1:14-16; 1 Thessalonians 5:22-24; Deuteronomy 22:5; Proverbs 18:21; Leviticus 20:13; Acts 10:34.

Discussion

1. What do you notice about the lifestyle of an individual who really commits to serving Yah?

2. What do you understand by the words: Holy, Sanctified, separated and consecrated?

3. What is the difference between the words righteous and holy?

4. How can we practically practice holiness in our life?

5. What is the one thing that you will take away from this lesson and use?

BREAD OF THE WORD COURSE TEST

1. What is repentance?

A. A change of mind, feelings and actions leading to a turning away from sin and toward Elohim?

B. Deciding to stop sinning?

C. Being sorry for sin and crying sincerely?

D. Confessing your sins to the Pastor or preacher?

2. Are Dead Works things one does :-

A. Before one is saved?

B. When not feeling very well?

C. A special class of sins?

D. Actions leading to death?

3. Being Holy means :-

A. To have a special type of personal atmosphere?

B. To be separate as Elohim is separate?

C. To be perfect in every way?

D. To dress correctly with no make up or jewelry?

4. Prayer is :

A. A set pattern of words that we must learn and repeat

every time we want Elohim's attention?

B. A special religious method or tone of talking to Elohim?

C. Talking to Elohim and letting Elohim talk to you?

D. A special language that only certain special people are able to speak to Elohim.

5. **Tithing means giving :-**

A. Half of everything you own to the Church?

B. One tenth of your income to the Pastor?

C. A good love offering when it is collection time, for the upkeep of the Pastor?

D. One tenth of all your income to Yah by giving it to the Church for the upkeep of the Ministry ?

6. **Jesus Messiah could be identified as :-**

A. A man who was just a prophet?

B. Elohim the son?

C. Almighty Elohim in a body?

D. The Archangel Michael manifested in the flesh?

7. **When a Christian is attacked by illness, their first response should be:**

A. Ring the Pastor immediately no matter how serious the complaint?

B. Take a tablet and say a prayer?

C. Ring or visit the Doctor or hospital immediately?

D. Pray for yourself first, and then call for the Elders of the Church to come and pray for you if you believe you need their special ministry?

8. **The correct way to view the Godhead (or who Elohim is) can be stated as:-**

A. The Elohim consciousness that is within each of us which leads us to make the most of ourselves and our capacity to explore the infinite?

B. There are three co-equal, co-eternal, co-assent persons that make one Elohim?

C. There are two Elohims; Yah the Almighty and His son Yahoshuah whom He created?

D. There is but one Father who is Elohim, who is a Holy Spirit, that put on flesh as the man Messiah Yahoshuah, but still remained one in totality and cannot be separated in number or person?

9. **The four foundation stones of a Good relationship are :**

A. Physical love, sympathy, trust, and understanding?

B. love, faith, respect, and understanding?

C. Trust, sympathy, frankness, and sincerity?

D. Love, friendliness, peacemaking, and negotiation?

10. **The most effective way to witness is :-**

A. To tell people what you think is wrong with their

life ?

B. Preach to everyone you meet about going to Hell?

C. To tell those around you the Gospel message when you feel led to?

D. Tell what Elohim has done for you, and support it with an exemplary life and comment that Elohim wants to do the same for everyone?

11. **The right to be a witness for Yahoshuah is decided by :-**

A. Having received the Holy Spirit and coming to know Him?

B. Having attended Church for a certain period of time?

C. Earning the right to witness by studying a lot?

D. A natural talent to speak to other people?

12. **What will change when Yahoshuah returns for his Church is :-**

A. Everything about us, mind, body, and spirit?

B. Man's spirit will be born again and people will go to be with the Yah?

C. Our bodies only will change to be like Yahoshuah'?

D. The attitudes of men towards Elohim and toward each other will change?

13. Faith can be defined as:-

A. Remembering what Elohim says in his word and hoping he will give it to you?

B. Remembering what Elohim has said in his word and taking him at his word, by trusting him to do it now for you?

C. To continually quote scripture to yourself optimistically?

D. To expect Elohim to do something when you need it, as long as you believe?

14. Being righteous means:-

A. Having the legal right to stand in the presence of Elohim boldly as a Son?

B. To be very good and do very little that is wrong in Elohim's sight?

C. To get more and more holy everyday by doing right?

D. Doing no wrong whatsoever?

15. In order to be saved, one must :-

A. Repent of sin, be baptised in the name of the Father, and of the Son and of the Holy Ghost, and receive the Holy Spirit; living on for Elohim.

B. Repent of sin, believe in the heart and confess with the mouth Yah Yahoshuah the Messiah, receive the baptism of the Holy Spirit if you want it and continue in Elohim's grace.

C. Repent of sin, be baptised in the name of Yahoshuah, receive the Holy Spirit with evidence of speaking in another Language by the power of Elohim and continue to live for Elohim.

D. Repent of sin, be baptised in the name of the Father and of the Son, and of the Holy Ghost in Yahoshuah's name, receive the Holy Ghost and continue living for Elohim.

16. **T/F**   Repentance is not necessary to be saved, so long as you are sincere?

17. **T/F**   Believing in one Elohim is the second most important command of the Bible?

18. **T/F**   Even though you are not living completely holy, you can still go to heaven to be with Yahoshuah when he comes for his church?

19. **T/F**   It is possible for a person to receive the Holy Spirit without the sign following of speaking in tongues?

20. **T/F**   Fasting is only for special Christians or special occasions, therefore it is   alright not to fast regularly on a personal basis?

21. **T/F**   The resurrection from the dead of Yahoshuah Messiah and the resurrection from the dead of the dead in Messiah that is prophesied are not actual physical occurrences, but are instead spiritual happenings?

22. **T/F**   The Bible is a book written by Elohim through men and by men?

Answers to questions asked

1. A;	12. C;
2. D;	13.B;
3. B;	14. A;
4. C;	15. C;
5. D;	16. F;
6. C;	17. F;
7. D;	18. F;
8. D;	19. F;
9. B;	20. F.
10. D;	21. F
11. A;	22. T

Corrective Actions

Result	Action
11 questions or less right = to 50% or less	Please re-read the entire book, you didn't get it.
13-15 right = 60-70%	Re-read all of the chapters

	covered by the questions you got wrong
17 or more questions right you did good with 80%	Be diligent to look at why you got those particular questions wrong that you did?
19-20 questions mean you are doing 90% or better	You done well, be pleased and correct the things that you got wrong.
All 22 questions right, you have done excellently AT 100%	Share what you have done with someone you care about and then teach someone else what you have learned

Bibliography

1. Paterson, John; God in Jesus Christ, Word Aflame press, Hazlewood, MO, 1966

2. Gordon, Bob; The foundations of christian living, Sovereign world, Chichester, England, 1988

3. Bernard David, The oneness of God, Word Aflame press, Hazlewood, MO, 1983

4. Erickson Gary, The conversion experience, Word Aflame press, Hazlewood, MO, 1987

5. Coon, Crawford D, Christian development course, Christian development publications, Alexandria, LA, 1987

6. McClure, P.T, Know the truth, McClure publishing, Melbourne FL, 1991

7. Rohn E, The pentecostal home study course, Pentecostal publishing house, Hazlewood MO, 1966

8. Eaton Michael, How to live a godly life, Sovereign World, Chichester, England, 1993

9. Jones Clifton, The prayer clinic manual, Bethesda Ministries, Fairfield OH, 2002

10. Smth Ron, Hoe Evangelism, Fishers fellowship, Waynesboro, GA, 1984

11. Burford P.D., et al, Facing the issues, Word Aflame press, Hazlewood, MO, 1992

12. Marshall, Tom, Understanding leadership, Sovereign world, Chichester, England, 1991

13. Arthur, Kay; Arthur, David; DeLacy, Pete; How to study your Bible, Harvest house publishers, 1994

14. McQuay, Chris; Broken Vessels, First Apostolic Church, Tinley Park, IL, 1987

15. Knight, Trevr F; Youth life (Spring cottage); Leeds, England, 1992

16. Urshan, Andrew Bar David; The supreme need of the hour,, Apostolic book publishers, Ivanhoe, OR, 1985

17. Griffi, Kelsey et al, Why a study of Christian standards, Word Aflame press, Hazlewood, MO, 1984

18. Douglas, Ken; How to pray people through to the Holy Ghost, Team Press, Del City, Oklaoma, 2009

19. Prime, Derek; Active Evangelism, Christian Focus, Ross-shire, Scotland, 2003

20. Rusthoi, Ralph W; Soulwinning course, McBeth Corporation, Chambersburg, PA, 1960

21. Pugh, JT; How to receive the Holy Ghost, Pentecostal publishing house, Hazlewood, MO, 1969

22. Cousen, Cecil; The curse of the law, Torbay publishing, Devon, England, 1987

23. Calver, Clive Et al, A guide to Evangelism, Marshalls paperbacks, Basingstoke, England, 1984

24. Wilkinson, Bruce; Boa, Kenneth; Talk thru the Bible, Thomas Nelson publishers, Nashville, TN, 1980

25. Berg Jeff and Burgess, Jim; The debt free church, Moody Press, Chicago, Il, 1996

26. Johns, Darrin J; Foundations of truth discipleship course, Calvary Pentecostal church, FL, 2002

27. Roberts, Oral; Miracle of seed faith, OREA publishing, Tulsa, OK, 1970

28. Smith, Larry; Rightly dividing the Word, Larry Smith publishing, El Campo, TX, 1979

29. Home missions division of UPCI, Lets have revival, Hazlewood, MO, 1982

30. Robertson, Noman; Tithing, Norman Robertson media, Matthews, NC, 1994

31. Smethurst, Dave; Equipped to go, Sovereign world, Chichester, England, 1991

74589231R00192

Made in the USA
Columbia, SC
06 August 2017